D1586428

The
Radical Approach

Papers on an
independent
Scotland

Copyright authors © 1976

Cased ISBN 0 905470 01
Paperback ISBN 0 905470 00 1

Cover design: Russell Bruce
Published by Palingenesis Press Ltd.
56 Dean Street, Edinburgh, EH4 1LQ

Printed by Lindsay & Co. Ltd.
17 Blackfriars Street, Edinburgh

FOREWORD
Margo MacDonald

When Gavin Kennedy first mentioned to me the idea of collecting a number of papers on the radical alternative open to Scotland, I thought: "Great. This will be one in the eye for those who think that ownership of a Labour Party membership card automatically corners the market in Internationalism, Fraternalism, Humanitarianism and so on and so on."

My next thought was that I really wanted to read the distilled, current thoughts of friends with whom I have worked and argued in unheated committee rooms and overheated kitchens and living rooms. I have not been disappointed. Although I correctly anticipated what some of my closest colleagues would write, and conclude, I still find new thoughts and variations on some well-polished themes.

This, I think is the principal merit in this collection of papers: it is an exposition of where its writers are now and it is a springboard for the further development of their attitudes and visions. The papers were never intended as a "blueprint to cure Scotland's problems". There are obvious gaps in the topics covered, and I trust that the next collection of papers will seek to remedy this, but at least they identify Scotland's challenges.

Perhaps it is in this eagerness to meet the challenge of Independence rather than in wasted determination to solve the congenital problems of the Scottish Region which distinguishes the Nationalist from the Devolutionist, the Radical from the Conservative.

The papers hold out hope for the kind of Scotland we can build, and they should go some way to allaying the fears of those faint-hearts, and Devolutionists, amongst us who dread the loss of London's overbearing influence.

Finally, my thanks and congratulations to all of the contributors: they did not break the ground, but they have planted the seeds.

CONTENTS

CONTRIBUTORS

Stephen Maxwell, formerly of the Institute of International Affairs, is S.N.P. Press Officer and a Lothian Region Councillor.

Isobel Lindsay, Lecturer in Sociology at Strathclyde University and Vice-Chairman (Policy) of the S.N.P.

Howie Firth, teacher, S.N.P. prospective parliamentary candidate for Orkney and Shetland and elected member of the S.N.P. National Council.

Andrew Currie, S.N.P. prospective parliamentary candidate for West Aberdeen and member of S.N.P. Transport Policy Committee.

Gavin Kennedy, Senior Lecturer in Economics at Strathclyde University and author of *The Economics of Defence*, London 1975.

David Simpson, Professor of Economics and Director of Fraser of Allander Institute at Strathclyde University and author of *General Equilibrium Analysis*, Oxford 1975.

David Hamilton, surgeon, member of the S.N.P. Health Policy Committee.

Colin Bell, journalist, S.N.P. prospective parliamentary candidate and member of the Housing Policy Committee.

David Purves, scientist, Convener of S.N.P. Environment Policy Committee.

Peter Craigie, consultant, Chairman of S.N.P. Edinburgh Central Constituency Association.

Owen Dudley Edwards, Lecturer in History, Edinburgh University, and author of *The Sins of Our Fathers* and several other books.

INTRODUCTION

The political situation in Scotland is on the boil. New possibilities of major, and long overdue, change are emerging as hundreds of thousands of Scots reconsider their political loyalties. The internal condition of the old Unionist parties is demoralising their activists and discouraging their supporters. The Scottish National Party stands as the single indicator of hope amidst the unrelieved gloom of current British political life.

Many thousands of Labour Party members have been confused, and not a little dismayed, by their party's tortured resistance to the idea of a Scottish Assembly. A couple of thousand supporters left and formed a new Scottish Labour Party (S.L.P.). The original White Paper proposals on devolution, which were apparently acceptable to even long-time devolutionists such as Labourite John Mackintosh, M.P., in December 1975, have been rejected as not strong enough in April 1976. True, this rejection was motivated more by political expediency — to cut off further defections to the S.L.P. — than conviction, as Willie Hamilton, M.P., tactlessly reminded us. The fact remains that even the new proposals of the Labour Party (Scottish Council) fall far short of the needs of the Scottish people. Whether the S.L.P. will take the next logical step and come out for independence remains to be seen.

It would be an error to claim that the Scots are a socialist electorate. The political power of the Labour Party rests on a minority of the voters and is heavily concentrated in West Central Scotland. But it would be a greater error to conclude that Labour and socialism are unimportant in Scotland. No amount of juggling of the arithmetic can produce a credible majority of parliamentary seats for independence that does not include substantial numbers of former Labour seats.

This was the central lesson of the 1974 elections. For the S.N.P., the tantalising prospect of independence is kept out of reach for the moment by 35 second places to Labour. Conversely, the prospects of another Labour Government at Westminster are threatened by the S.N.P. Thus, the central political struggle in Scotland is now between Labour and the S.N.P.

Impending events cast their shadows before them. The increasingly bitter, and regrettably hysterical, confrontation of Labour and S.N.P. is one manifestation of the realisation of what is at stake. Savage and emotional attacks on the S.N.P. are being made with increasing frequency by Labourite M.Ps. Nothing unites a rancorous and divided meeting of Labourites more than a vicious attack on the S.N.P.

Intellectuals usually feel the need to explain themselves. In Scotland this took the form in early 1975 of *The Red Paper on Scotland*.[1] It is inevitable that some people will regard this volume as, in some way, a reply to that publication. That would flatter both books. The genesis of *The Red Paper* can be found in the profound political shake-up inside the Labour Party after 1974. Socialists within the Labour Party came up against a major contradiction in their political philosophy regarding their opposition to nationalism in their own country.

Over the years, thousands of Labourites have marched, demonstrated and

1

demanded independence for scores of countries all round the world. Many of them have sympathised with the cause of Irish nationalism. Many of them opposed British entry into the E.E.C. on the grounds of the national interests of the U.K. and a desire to fight the multinationals. Their suspicions of the E.E.C. led them to chauvinistic stances that would not have disgraced the League of Empire Loyalists.

Great political events concentrate the minds of those who live through them. The experience of eight Labour Governments has shaken the credulity of all but the most opportunistic of Labourites when set against the hopes of a movement founded to redress injustice, redistribute income and reassign social and economic priorities.[2] In Scotland, that wasteland of Labour's hopes, the inevitable failure to deal with the pressing social and economic problems within the context of a British "solution" raises questions which the Labour movement cannot avoid. Thus, *The Red Paper* was produced to assuage doubts about the efficacy of Labour's position on self-government.

Events have moved on for the authors of *The Red Paper*. Some of them have made the logical step from the British connection towards the Scottish dimension. But if the S.L.P. has regrouped some of the authors the Stalinists in the Scottish Council of the Labour Party have made moves to block off the advance of the national movement. We are being treated at present to practice runs of the propaganda of defamation, hatred and deceit. This will increase in crescendo in step with the march towards the General Election.

This volume then is not a reply to *The Red Paper*. The time for that has gone past. It is a contribution to the debate that began with the political changes of 1974. It is the first of several addresses to the political debate. The authors have written as individuals. All of them are committed members of the S.N.P., all of them are among the working activists of the national movement, none of them are armchair philosophers.

The urgency of the debate now going on in Scotland dominated the time allowed to get this first volume off the presses. This has meant that many important topics have not been covered in this volume. For example, education, poverty, external affairs, law reform, defence, fisheries, planning, industrial development and local government are among the many subjects not covered. These will be published in a subsequent volume as *Further Papers on an Independent Scotland*.

The authors have written their papers without consultation with each other and without editorial meetings to tune into a party line. This is one of the remarkable features of this collection. That eleven authors, in a party that is accused by its opponents of having no political philosophy and no consensus on policies, can produce, independently of each other, a set of papers that have managed to combine a broadly definable political viewpoint and an individual approach to issues is an excellent advertisement for the genuine radicalism and integrity of the S.N.P.

Stephen Maxwell's paper on social democracy is an important statement on the dangers of the corporate state which is being created in Labour Britain. That Labour Britain is bringing to fruition the great dreams of Italian *fascism*, albeit with the best of intentions, is one of politic's ironies.[3] That it is alien to the motivations of Scottish nationalism is the best place to begin the radical contribution to the debate on Scottish independence.

2

Isobel Lindsay takes the argument about community and democracy a step or two further. People in Scotland are as likely, if not more likely, to be dominated by the powers and privileges of state corporations as they are by private monopolies. Nationalists reject the substitution of private corporate monopolies by state monopolies that leave the employees, the managed, the consumer and the community in exactly the same position in relation to the power brokers as they were before. Her point that our opponents understand our criticism and react against us because they aspire to the powerful bureaucracies we intend to break up is especially perceptive. For those socialists who have misunderstood our criticism up to now this is a fine opportunity to test the integrity of their libertarian intentions.

Howie Firth and Andrew Currie take up the issues of balanced development in the Orkney and Shetland communities and the Highlands and Islands. No reading of these papers could possibly provide evidence that the S.N.P. is in the pocket of lairds, landowners and property speculators. Orkney and Shetland need an opportunity to develop a balanced economy that enhances the quality of life of their communities. Their current dependence on the extended market economy of the mainland can only be reversed by Scottish independence. Oil plus the British connection cannot provide a solution that will last beyond the oil. Devolving power to the communities and allowing them to set the terms for the exploitation of natural resources are essential elements to self-realisation. An independent Scotland in granting autonomy to Orkney and Shetland will do so because it is an extension of its political philosophy and not because of the black gold.

Andrew Currie's paper on the Highland "problem" is one of the most deeply thought out pieces on this subject that has been written for many years. The central government reaction to any economic and social problem is to set up an institution to dispense cash. Once again the solution lies in community-centred development, under local control, and based on a thorough understanding of the life-styles of the people rather than on projections of the problems, or solutions, of the urban centres.

The economy is discussed in the editor's own paper. The central point must be that there is no question of living standards falling. This removes the economic argument against self-government. David Simpson makes proposals that will solve the vexed question of the disposal of oil revenues and the oil itself. The S.N.P. is often accused of being selfish with regard to the oil. This is unjust. The S.N.P. has demanded Scottish political sovereignty over the oil in Scottish waters in exactly the same way as the Zambians have demanded political sovereignty over their copper. The right of a country to control the extraction, processing and disposal of natural resources is a fundamental right of nations throughout the world.

The charge of selfishness and the politics of greed, it must be remembered, come from the British whose whole economy is based on the selfish extraction of other peoples' natural resources. Britain maintains its standard of living by borrowing from international banks and paying cheap prices for imported raw materials. A surge in prices is necessary in these commodities if the poor, not to say wretched, producers are to reach living standards above that of subsistence.[4]

Scotland does not need to exploit anybody and seeks no empires, commercial or otherwise. It does not need to drain scarce food resources away from other countries as England does and can pay its way in the world for what it needs at prices that guarantee a hope of life for those driven into world markets to sell their precious natural heritage. David Purves in his paper may take an extreme view on this subject for some people but his basic message is clear: either the industrialised change their ways or they will reap the whirlwind. Scottish independence is the most unselfish act that the Scots can vote for; the British connection is the exact opposite.

The papers by David Hamilton and Colin Bell deal with two of the three most important institutional services of the welfare society, health and housing. Education, as mentioned above, will be dealt with in the next volume of papers. David Hamilton makes the case for a Scottish health service that serves the people and is democratically administered by *all* who work in it. Much of what he argues for has already passed into S.N.P. official policy which is itself a testament for the humanitarian commitment of nationalism. Radical nationalists want a national, publicly financed and controlled health service that begins with the principles of the old N.H.S. but rejects the bureaucratic stifling of humanity and effectiveness that pervades the current system. On housing, Colin Bell argues for a non-doctrinaire approach that provides people with homes that are worth living in instead of housing schemes, built on borrowed money, that are not fit in any real sense for *human* habitation. Labour and Tory doctrinal theories on housing have made a mockery of the socially just society; Labour in particular have created housing ghettoes in Scotland and their only virtue is to corral a Labour vote. The Tories have tolerated speculation in private housing, much of it of deplorable quality, and reacted with callous indifference to the miseries perpetrated on urban and rural Scots by inadequate housing, bullying landlords and stone-faced profiteers. Colin Bell's radical proposals deserve serious study by all who are genuinely committed to resolving the Scottish housing problem once and for all.

Peter Craigie makes a stab at the problem of industrial relations. His paper links up well with the proposals from Stephen Maxwell for democratically managed enterprises. The paper does not make the mistake of wishing for eternal peace and tranquillity in industry and recognises at the start the socially necessary role of inter-group conflict. Reforms based on altering the power structure of management to include the managed are part of a general assault on inequalities in wealth and income. Peter Craigie's proposals may not meet with immediate approval from the trade unions and the currently dominant management groups but that they are in the right direction is evidenced by trends in Western industry all over Europe and North America. The big problem for industrial democracy is not the efficacy of the proposition but the inability of the corporate state to co-exist with a devolved and democratic control of the resource base of society.

The last paper in this volume is by Owen Dudley Edwards on Socialism or Nationalism? Unlike other authors, Owen Dudley Edwards declares himself a socialist and a nationalist. (His supposition that his colleagues are in the main in some way socialist by persuasion is an unsolicited testimonial that some of them may object to). The Editor gladly joins Owen in a declaration of commitment to socialism. There is no need to hide commitment to political philosophy in the S.N.P. The party has many political persuasions, and tendencies within persua-

4

sions, in its ranks. The S.N.P. itself is *not* a socialist party and has never pretended to be other than a national party seeking self-government.

The Tories are ever keen to find proof that the S.N.P. is a socialist party; Labour is just as keen to prove it is conservative. The media is even keener to find evidence of splits. Even some S.N.P. members are overly sensitive on the issue of public debate. No great movement for meaningful change can hope to advance towards its goal without internal controversy. The S.N.P. in order to get the majority it needs for independence will inevitably bring into its ranks many thousands of active members who were formerly in other political parties. This will enrich the party. The recruits will also be enriched by exposure to people of different ideologies and different beliefs. I am sure Owen Dudley Edwards would agree that his socialism has been enriched by membership of the national party. This has certainly been the experience of the Editor. The basic decency of the S.N.P. membership, their sheer honesty and integrity, and their absolute commitment to the good of their country is the best guarantee that Stalinist tendencies in socialism and capitalism (which fuse in the corporate state) have no chance of emerging.

What will be the political shape of an independent Scotland? There are no clues to be found in a scrutiny of the minutia of S.N.P. policy statements, or in the political philosophies of S.N.P. members, or indeed, in the papers in this volume. Post-independence Scotland has yet to be fought for and much will depend on what is going on in the world at the time.

Some on the Left believe the British connection gives them the best chance of realising their goal of socialism on the Stalinist/Trotskyist model. They are counterbalanced by some people on the Right who believe the British connection is the best guarantee of the preservation of capitalism. A few on the extreme Left have opted for independence and a workers' republic.

For radical nationalists the future of Scotland is bound up by the extent to which the ideas and approach of this, and subsequent, volumes are taken up by the people of Scotland. Radicals approach independence with a great deal of optimism and a granite determination to influence the future of their country. Independence for Scotland is on the agenda and nationalists intend to keep it there until we can pass over to the post-independence reconstruction of our country. This is no job for faint hearts serving trivial ends. Neither is the S.N.P. a place for opportunists and carpet baggers. Our country requires more of us than we can give but independence will give our people more than they can hope for. It is for this that these papers have been written.

Gavin Kennedy
Edinburgh, April 1976

1 Gordon Brown, editor, *The Red Paper on Scotland*, Edinburgh 1975.
2 See, for instance Thomas Johnston, *The History of the Working Classes in Scotland*, Glasgow, 1920; published four years before the first of Labour's eight British governments.
3 Note Anthony Wedgewood Benn's speech to the Scottish Trades Union Conference in Perth, April 1976 and his call on the trade unions to take up their responsibilities in the corporate state. For an account of the intellectual origins of the corporate state see Adrian Lyttelton, *Italian Fascisms: from Pareto to Gentile*, London 1973.
4 Gustav Ranis, editor, *The Gap Between the Rich and Poor Nations*, London, 1972.

BEYOND SOCIAL DEMOCRACY

Stephen Maxwell

The Scottish National Party has traditionally rejected any ideological label which would fix its position on the conventional Left-Right spectrum. The reasons are partly opportunistic and partly a matter of principle. In the Party's early years a strong body of opinion argued that the S.N.P.'s role should be to act as an umbrella under which all who believed in Scotland's independence, whatever their social or economic beliefs, could unite. The implication was that the Party would dissolve on the attainment of independence, freeing its members to rejoin the political organisation of their ideological choice. By the early 1960's, the gestation period of the modern S.N.P., this position was a minority one within the Party, although the acute S.N.P. listener may still detect echoes of the argument today.

A second and perhaps more important reason behind the S.N.P.'s rejection of a conventional ideological label was a belief that the S.N.P. represented a distinctive Scottish way in politics. It can be identified in the occasional writings and the recorded speeches of S.N.P. activists over the last several decades. Its point of departure is the myth of Scottish Democracy, which is seen as rejecting class theories of politics, as being anti-bureaucratic and egalitarian with strong populist overtones and placing great emphasis on the value of local and community identity. To some extent, indeed, it reflects the small-town ethos of the pioneers of the S.N.P. In recent years it has been mixed, rather uncertainly, with more fashionable ideas of decentralisation, the value of what is small in scale, a belief in the need to restore *communitas* as an antidote to the alienation created by mass industrial society and even with conservationist ideas.

As the S.N.P.'s electoral support and its prospect of governmental responsibility have grown the Party has felt impelled to define more closely its position on a wide range of social and economic issues. In the process it has explicitly rejected an umbrella role. It has stated its ambition to provide not merely a vehicle for a broad movement for independence, but to form the future government of an independent Scotland. At the same time, it has relaxed its opposition to conventional political labelling. Following the February 1974 General Election some S.N.P. spokesmen for the first time publicly identified S.N.P. as a social democratic party and the Party's October 1974 Election Manifesto claimed to outline a comprehensive programme of "social democracy". Since October 1974 the S.N.P.'s social democratic claims have been restated in public by leading S.N.P. members[1] and have been the subject of discussion within the Party.

Why has the social democratic label proved acceptable to large sections of a Party that has traditionally rejected ideological labels? Social democracy is consistent with S.N.P.'s non-ideological tradition only to the extent that in its contemporary meaning it implies a rejection of the ideological stereotypes of socialism and laisser-faire capitalism. Partly for that reason it carries a public relations gloss of moderation and even of conservatism which is convenient to a Party which is proposing a major constitutional upheaval. It also sounds Scandinavian and S.N.P. opinion is agreed on the merit of things Scandinavian. Cynics may suspect that its acceptability is further enhanced by its vagueness. Certainly none of those within the S.N.P. who have declared themselves social democrats have yet offered a systematic account of what they understand by the phrase.

What is Social Democracy?

Generically social democracy denotes a belief that social and economic justice should be pursued within a framework of democracy, liberty and the rule of law.[2] Such a belief, however, fails to distinguish the social democrat from the democratic socialist or the Liberal or even the progressive Tory. Historically social democracy describes the democratic Parliamentary road to socialism advocated by nineteenth-century German Marxist revisionists like Edward Bernstein. In the twentieth century, however, social democracy has been drained of much of its socialist content until today the most ardent socialists use the label "social democrat" to abuse the right wing of the Labour movement.

The main area of disagreement between socialist and social democrat concerns the role of public ownership of the means of production. Anthony Crosland considers public ownership—which he sees exclusively in terms of nationalisation—as no more than "one of the instruments available to government to deal with excessive monopoly power, or consistent under-investment or (as in the case of oil or minerals or development land) a failure to plan a national resource in the interests of the community". He congratulates the Swedish, West German and Austrian social democratic parties for their ideological indifference to the issue of public ownership.[3]

In upholding the case for the mixed economy, social democrats intend a challenge to the traditional socialist belief that public ownership is the key to the achievement of such socialist objectives as equality, full employment and the elimination of poverty. In their view these objectives can be achieved through a combination of social legislation. public expenditure and the use by the state of its powers of control over the private sector. Consistent with this they evince little interest in exploring alternatives to the state corporation model of public or social ownership. A commitment to industrial democracy is usually all that remains of the classic socialist aim of the elimination of private ownership.

The social democratic belief in the virtues of the mixed economy is accompanied by a commitment to public expenditure through the welfare state as the chief instrument for the achievement of social objectives. In health and education the social democratic welfare state embraces the socialist principle of universal flat rate benefits. In the case of personal income support and family welfare, however, the welfare state in its British form offers a mixture of universal, selective and graduated benefits. Universal flat-rate family allowance exist side-by-side with selective, means-tested, free school meals and supplementary benefits, and with graduated unemployment and retirement benefits.

Since the 1930s social democracy has been virtually synonymous with Keynesian economics. Keynesian theories of economic management had the

8

great attraction for social democrats of offering an alternative to public owner-ship as a way of combating the recurring crises of capitalism and of ensuring full employment and steady economic growth.

The fifth tenet of social democracy is equality. Indeed today's social democrats seek to establish a rhetorical commitment to equality as the touchstone of socialism in place of the traditional commitment to public ownership. Anthony Crosland has written: "By equality we mean more than a meritocratic society of equal opportunities in which unequal rewards would be distributed to those most fortunate in their genetic endowments or family background. We also mean more than a simple redistribution of income. We want a wider social equality embracing the distribution of property, the educational system, social class relationships, power and privilege — indeed all that is enshrined in the age-old socialist dream of a 'classless society'."[4] Contemporary social democracy rests therefore on five tenets — political liberalism, the mixed economy, the welfare state, Keynesian economics and a belief in equality.

The Corporate State

As an organised and effective political force social democracy was largely the product of the Labour movement. The aims pursued by Labour's political wing — the improvement of the social conditions of the working class, the defence of the legal rights of trade unions and the creation of economic conditions which supported the bargaining power of labour against capital — were initially seen as steps *towards* socialism. But as the industrial and political pressure exerted by the Labour movement forced the state to recognise its claims, the movement began to distinguish its sectional interest from its universalist aims. It became, in brief, more "labourist" and less socialist and was confirmed in this tendency by the unsuspected capacity of the state, under the influence of social democratic ideas, to develop new means of meeting its demands.

Partly in response to continued pressure from the Labour movement, partly in response to broader electoral pressures, the initial achievements of the state generated the demand for further extensions of the state's role. The state's power to plan the economy was consolidated by the nationalisation of strategic industries. The need to limit the cost to the community of sustaining full employment drove the state to seek improvements in industrial productivity and efficiency through the elaboration of a range of state agencies and financial incentives designed to encourage rationalisation and restructuring. Having weakened, if not eliminated, the harsh discipline of the market by social democratic economic management, the state sought to substitute the gentler discipline of state sponsored incomes' policies. To meet the escalating administrative demands imposed by the growth in its responsibilities, the state spawned a bureaucracy whose power grew in proportion to the range and complexity of the tasks assigned to it, until it became a dominant — perhaps *the* dominant — political feature of the social democratic state.

The growth in the economic bargaining power and political influence of organised labour, and the extension of the state's role in the economy and society which it stimulated, provoked other interests to organise themselves in order to impress their sectional views on the attention of the state. The private sector of industry, which was anyway undergoing a secular process of concentration, had

9

the most obvious incentive to deploy a countervailing influence on the state, but other interests, from the British Medical Association and the National Farmers' Union to the Self-Employed, sought likewise to maximise their influence on state decisions. And while the Labour movement preserved its institutional solidarity, the broadening of its membership, in an increasingly specialised economy, to include large sections of non-manual and even middle class groups, served to emphasise the fact that the movement contained different, potentially rival, interests. Paradoxically, the social democratic state, built on the principle of society's collective responsibility for the welfare of the individual, has come to preside over a society of competing sectional interest groups.

Decisive power in the democratic state, however, lies with a triad of interests: a trade union movement which owes much of its power to the state while reserving an ultimate independence from it; a concentration of financial and industrial interests which has learned to see the state as a potential source of support in times of crisis, as well as a constant supervisory presence in normal times; and the state itself, acting in its administrative capacity with all the strength of an extensive and often impenetrable bureaucracy.

In its representative role the state, although in democratic theory the instrument of the collective will of this sectionalised society, has been forced to acknowledge severe limitations to its power. Sometimes it has been limited to holding the ring while competing interests bargained to determine their share of society's resources: sometimes it has accepted the role of *primus inter pares,* treating sectional interests at one moment as rivals in a hard-bargaining process, at another as partners. The close relationship which has developed between the executive and bureaucratic organs of the state and the leadership of the major sectional interests, above all the Labour movement, forms the skeleton of the Corporate State.

Compounding these corporatist tendencies, social democratic orthodoxy has tended to pursue political integration alongside economic integration. It has been an axiom of social democracy that whatever is bigger is best. For example, support for rationalisation in the economic field has been paralleled in the political field by the reform of local government to create larger and putatively more efficient units and by advocacy of political integration at the level of the E.E.C. In the U.K., E.E.C. membership has the support of virtually all leading social democrats. In the Scandinavian countries opposition to the E.E.C. has come from populist and parochial interests, and dissident intellectual groups, outwith the consensus built around Labour/Social Democratic parties and the trade union establishment.

Failures of Social Democracy

Today both the doctrines of social democracy and the structure of power characteristic of the social democratic state are under attack. The assumptions and techniques of centralised Keynesian economic management are proving incapable of reconciling full employment with price stability. The introduction of incomes' policies represents the social democratic state's response to the dilemma, but while statutory policies have proved ineffectual due to union opposition, voluntary agreements have still to prove themselves.

The reduction in the rate of wages increases in the United Kingdom under the present Labour Government's incomes' policy may be due more to the

10

insecurity generated by the exceptional levels of unemployment than to trade union support for the policy on its merits. The real test of such voluntary agreements will come when the developed countries move out of recession into the next boom.

The social democratic state has also failed to eliminate poverty. In the United Kingdom according to one estimate, some 10 million people live on or close to the official poverty line as defined by the qualifying level for supplementary benefits.[5] In West Germany a pilot research project in Dortmund has revealed the existence of a significant amount of submerged poverty.[6] A commentator on the Level of Living studies being carried out in the Nordic countries has concluded that "fairly substantial groups — in particular in new urban residential areas and among the old — are unable to meet everyday needs even with apparently reasonable incomes"[7] What is more, in spite of the survival of poverty in the growth years of the 1950s and early 1960s, and the doubtful prospects for sustained growth in the immediate future, many social democrats remain committed to the view that resources needed for the elimination of poverty can come only from economic growth.

Social democracy is nowhere more ambivalent than in the way it interprets its much advertised commitment to equality. The social democrat's tolerance of a private sector of education alongside a comprehensive state system may be understood as his proper homage to liberalism. But the persistent reluctance to take action deliberately to reduce differences of income and of wealth beyond certain generous limits cannot be explained so conveniently by a tension between different values within the social democratic credo. Fourteen years of social democratic government since the war have left the United Kingdom still a notably unequal and class-ridden society. Indeed Denis Healey, social democratic Chancellor of the Exchequer, apparently believes that even the present range of inequalities of income, and the even greater differences in standards of living, gives an inadequate incentive to the middle class.

In most social democracies the balance between the public sector and the private sector in the economy has been eroded by the continued expansion of public sector employment and by the increasing proportion of national income going on public expenditure. Some social democrats now believe that further increases in the share of national income going to public expenditure will seriously endanger the individual's freedom of economic choice,[8] but as long as this simplistic view is held it will serve to restrain the growth of expenditure in many areas in which social democracy has patently failed to achieve its social objectives.

Although social democracy officially endorses the claims of political liberalism, it has not been conspicuously fertile in ideas for curtailing the growth in state power or for protecting the citizen against its misuse. Anti-discrimination legislation apart, social democratic concern for individual rights has been concentrated on the rights of employees in respect of their employers and has tended to relapse into ambivalence on the issue of the individual's rights in respect of the collective power of his trade union. Social democracy typically identifies the balance between private economic power on the one hand and individual rights or public power on the other as the crucial political relationship. The balance between central and local power, or individual rights (beyond the basic democratic freedoms) and state power, has been regarded as of secondary importance, with initiatives often depending on a leading politician's personal commitment or on acute electoral pressure.

Social democracy has, further, inherited from its trade union origins an instinct to concentrate its strength and to avoid particularist division, while the adoption of Keynesian techniques of aggregate economic managment has served to reinforce the dominant role of a powerful central state, as illustrated by the fact that social democracy's endorsement of regional policy has been firmly posited on the need for central administration. Further support for these centralist tendencies has come in the United Kingdom from the fact that the political leaders of social democracy have been drawn increasingly from an English middle class nurtured on the peculiarly English doctrine of Parliamentary sovereignty.

Social democracy's tattered record provides an ironic commentary on the claim that the S.N.P. represents a new form of politics: ". . . a contemporary social democracy . . . the realignment of all good Centre/Left men which the trendy leader writers keep calling for . . ."[9] An examination of the problems which will face an independent Scotland confirms that social democracy, at least as conventionally practised and preached in the United Kingdom, will prove an unreliable and even dangerous guide for Scottish legislators.

Scotland's Industrial Crisis

Scotland faces an industrial crisis composed of three main elements — an overdependence on traditional industries now in decline, an inadequate level of new investment and an exceptionally high level of foreign ownership. While independence will create an opportunity for sustained economic growth denied to Scotland as part of the United Kingdom such growth will not by itself solve these structural weaknesses.

In recognition of this the S.N.P. has accepted the need for wide-ranging state intervention in the Scottish economy supported by a massive programme of public sector investment through possible doubling of overall public expenditure in real terms over a five-year period. To implement this policy the S.N.P. has proposed a range of state agencies from Scottish boards for existing nationalised industries to a Scottish Industrial Development Corporation and State Holding Companies operating under a Ministry of Development and Industry.[10]

Scotland's long-term economic prospects cannot be made secure while the present degree of external control exists.[11] (Only 41% of Scotland's manufacturing labour force is employed by Scottish controlled firms.) S.N.P. has advocated a more selective attitude to the award of development incentives to foreign capital and the introduction of a system for monitoring threatened foreign takeovers of Scottish firms as of other forms of proposed foreign investment. But foreign capital is already so dominant in many key industries that direct intervention will be required if the Scottish economy is to develop a self-renewing base. The most direct form of intervention would be for a Scottish government to take a share in existing foreign-owned firms or to purchase them outright. Given the abundance of liquid finance available to a Scottish government in the form of oil revenues a systematic policy of repatriation of industrial control would pose no financial problem, though other considerations would dictate a gradual and selective approach.

These three key developments — a massive programme of public sector investment, the elaboration of new agencies of state intervention and the direct state purchase of foreign-controlled assets — measure in the industrial field the extent of the swing towards state dominance of the economy which must be expected in an independent Scotland in the absence of corrective policies.

Oil and the Mixed Economy

The accretion of power to a Scottish state is further illustrated by the financial implications of Scottish oil. In the United Kingdom at present public expenditure represents some 60 % of gross domestic product, which according to one leading English social democrat is the maximum compatible with reserving to the individual a proper freedom of choice.[12] Public expenditure, in Scotland, however, represents no less than 66% of Scotland's gross domestic product. At an annual production of 100 million tons, oil will be contributing some 36% of Scotland's total g.d.p. in 1980, assuming an annual 2.4% growth in non-oil g.d.p. If a Scottish government continued the present level of public expenditure and added to it the revenues yielded even by the London Government's modest 66% tax on the gross value of the oil, the resulting public expenditure at 66% of total g.d.p. would represent no less than 90.5% of the non-oil g.d.p. If public expenditure was increased by the revenues yielded by, say, a 75% tax on the oil (in line with S.N.P. plans), then it would represent close to 70% of total g.d.p. (and 94% of the non-oil g.d.p.).

Of course, the Scottish economy's limited capacity to absorb new resources means that a Scottish government would not wish to increase annual public expenditure by anything like the £3,000 million plus which oil taxation would yield. On different, and more realistic, assumptions, embracing an annual 9% growth in non-oil g.d.p. from 1980, an end to deficit financing and a lightening of the tax burden, the level of public expenditure could be reduced to 55% of non-oil g.d.p. by 1985 *while still allowing for a doubling of public expenditure in real terms.* While this reduction would meet the fears of some social democrats of the growth in public expenditure, both the extent and the manner of the reduction would be at the state's discretion, the reduction in effect being a substitution of oil financed expenditure for non-oil financed expenditure. At the same time the scope for increased public expenditure would continue to pose a threat to the industrial base of the mixed economy.

The task of sustaining a balance between the private and the public sectors of industry will be a difficult one for Scottish social democrats. The conventional instruments of development grants, tax incentives, the provision of infrastructure and of central research and advisory services, would almost certainly fail to overcome the exceptional weakness of the private sector. Native Scottish industry would be unable to absorb financial resources in the necessary volume or to compete successfully against foreign enterprises in exploiting the benefits of a higher rate of growth and of the new infrastructure. At the same time, social democracy's endorsement of economic integration within the Common Market would limit its ability to pursue the discriminatory measures which might redress the balance of advantage in favour of indigenous industries.

If, notwithstanding these obstacles, the new Scottish state were to persist in attempting to revive a large private sector through the lavish disbursement of public funds to private interests, it would be exposing politicians and administrators to the most intensive lobbying and pressure from the carpetbaggers, con men and speculators who would undoubtedly be attracted by the prospect of state handouts. The result would be a jerry-built private sector lacking sound foundations. In these circumstances social democracy could be expected to resort as a *pis aller* to the creation of more state corporations of a familiar kind so consolidating and intensifying the statist pattern of power which London control has already grafted on to Scottish society.

The Radical Alternative

The combination in an independent Scotland of a potentially overwhelming state power and a conspicuously weak private sector not only makes the social democratic model of a mixed economy dangerously inappropriate: it also challenges the S.N.P.'s commitment to the decentralisation of power. At the same time it creates an opportunity for a move towards a new pattern of economic power based on an alternative concept of the mixed economy. The social democratic concept describes a mix between centralised public ownership and a private sector which in practice is increasingly dominated by large corporations. The radical alternative is a mix between state corporations on the existing model and a combination of public ownership and decentralised social or employee control and ownership.

A variety of models of economic decentralisation, ranging from the conservative to the radical, offer themselves. The basic requirement, however, is that a Scottish government should make it a normal, if not necessarily an invariable, condition of any development grant, loan or tax concession that the favoured enterprise should be organised on democratic principles with decision taking power lying either with employees or with employee representatives and representatives of public bodies, preferably local, acting together.

In the conservative model, new industries could be encouraged through a partnership of the state, as the main source of capital, and workers' co-operatives. The state would have a share in control through a state holding company and its nominees on the board of the co-operative. The same formula of shared control could be applied to foreign firms bought back into Scottish control by the state and also, at local level, to democratically organised enterprises established by reformed and strengthened local authorities. A democratically organised industrial sector sponsored in this way by public bodies could co-exist with a private sector (and a nationalised sector), modified by whatever statutory forms of co-determination or employee participation might be considered appropriate. In an economy mixed in this way, some of the disadvantages under which new, democratically organised enterprises might find themselves in a market dominated by larger, often externally controlled, firms in the private sector could be reduced by fiscal and other measures favouring small firms[13] and by legal provision for the extension of employee control — and hence an element of local control — in all firms whose labour force exceeded a certain size.

The radical model of economic decentralisation is built on the transformation of private ownership and control into employee control through the statutory transfer of the voting rights of shareholders to the employees.[14] Share ownership where relevant could continue to draw an economic reward in the form of a dividend (or even of capital appreciation) but would no longer constitute a claim to a share in the collective decisions of the enterprise. The assets of enterprises might be entirely held by outside shareholders or they might be owned on co-operative principles by the employees themselves. Clearly this model assumes the continuation of a private capital market, which could be supplemented by state banks offering loans either at commercial interest rates or, in the case of "venture" capital or enterprises in development areas, at subsidised interest rates.

The case for employee sovereignty has recently been advocated as part of a strategy to restore to the market the central role in the allocation of resources denied it by social democratic economic management.[15] In this strategy, democratically organised units of production would compete for markets and investment in an economy in which the expansion of the money supply would be as large as — and no larger than — the growth in productive capacity warranted. Increases in money wages would not automatically be covered by inflationary increases in the money supply as the politically expedient short-term alternative to unemployment, and workers' control and ownership would impose a new sense of economic responsibility on the labour force.

As an alternative to the looming corporate state this picture of employee and consumer sovereignty has its attractions. But it assumes that the centralised bargaining power of the trade unions would be broken-up by the spread of dispersed centres of employee control and that elected governments would withstand the inevitable electoral pressures to accommodate their economic policies to premature or excessive demands for sectional increases in living standards. Both these assumptions are problematic. Whatever new economic policy options decentralisation of industrial control might uncover, it should be pursued in an independent Scotland in the first instance with the aim of limiting the growth of state power.

Redistribution of Wealth

The problem of poverty in Scotland poses an equally serious challenge to social democratic orthodoxy. The S.N.P.'s early estimate that one and a quarter million Scots were living on or close to the poverty line[16] has been supported by subsequent academic research.[17] An increased rate of economic growth, although it will certainly reduce poverty related to unemployment, will not be itself improve the situation of the majority of those living in poverty — those dependent on state support and the lower wage earners who often lack economic bargaining power even at times of economic expansion. Nor can it be assumed that the increased revenues available to a Scottish government as a result of the oil and a high rate of economic growth will allow a painless redistribution of wealth on the classic social democratic model. In the growth years of the 1950's and early 1960's the poor in the United Kingdom were denied an adequate share of the increasing wealth because more powerful interests pressed their own claims in the form of higher personal incomes or of increased public expenditure of which they were themselves often the chief beneficiaries.

The expanding wealth of an independent Scotland will be no less subject to competing claims. The demands for increased industrial investment have already been noted and if the movement for independence does indeed represent a "revolution of rising expectations" as some commentators plausibly suggest, independence can be expected to release an enormous pent-up demand for the higher standard of living of the south-east of England, or the even higher ones of Scandinavia or Switzerland, which S.N.P. propaganda has encouraged them to anticipate. Even if the social democratic consensus were to prove itself capable of securing, against the competing claims of powerfully organised sectional interests, the volume of resources required to eliminate poverty, the welfare state has been shown to be an imperfect instrument for distributing resources to those most in need. It may prove particularly ill-equipped to meet the problem of the relative poverty which will be constantly recreated in the dynamic, expanding economy of an independent Scotland.

The best hope of eliminating poverty in Scotland lies, not in any selective attempt to repair the many holes in the welfare state net, but in a combination of an expanded programme of environmental improvement, including housing, and the introduction of a national minimum income or social dividend set at a generous proportion of the median wage. Automatic entitlement, on a non-contributory basis, would extend to pensioners, the disabled, the unemployed and to all those of working age who are excluded from the labour market by responsibility for dependants. Single parents, those engaged in the full-time private care of the elderly and infirm and whichever partner accepted primary responsibility for the home and care of children would all thus be eligible. Such a reform would dramatically strengthen the economic position of women by removing the mother's dependence on a breadwinner, and would thus contribute more to women's liberation than volumes of anti-discrimination legislation. The eventual extension of a guaranteed basic income to those who chose to opt out of the labour market for no other reason than to do their own thing, would mark a further step towards a libertarian, civilised society.[18]

The raising of Scotland's "forgotten fifth" out of poverty through a guaranteed income would not transform Scotland into an egalitarian society. Although differences of income are slightly less marked in Scotland than in England this is due mainly to the under representation of Scotland in the senior executive and managerial groups,[19] a state of affairs which the economic consequences of independence could be expected to correct.

A recent report of the Royal Commission on the Distribution of Income and Wealth has confirmed that personal wealth is to a significant degree more unevenly distributed in Scotland than in England.[20] The wealthiest one per cent own 27.6% of personal wealth in England and Wales, but 32.2% in Scotland, while the top 5% own 62.8% in Scotland against 50.4% in England. Such inequality, however much it may be condemned in the official rhetoric of social democracy, does not appear to be intolerably offensive to social democrats in government. It remains to be seen whether in response to the new political opportunities of independence, the egalitarianism which is one element in the myth of Scottish Democracy will inspire a radical attack on such inequalities.

Sectional Demands

In the determination of this issue, as of the minimum income guarantee and the overall social and economic prospects of an independent Scotland, the role of the more powerful sectional interests will be as crucial as it is to the current prospects of the United Kingdom. It promises to be no less problematical. Even with oil the resources of an independent Scotland will be under serious strain. The massively increased programmes of industrial investment and the

16

lightening of the tax burden will make heavy demands on economic capacity, while the increased rate of economic growth will generate its own upward pull on incomes. If, in addition, a minimum income guarantee were introduced, it would not only represent a further demand on resources but would threaten the traditional range of income differentials in one of its most sensitive areas — where the skilled worker compares his reward to that of the unskilled worker or the non-worker. If powerful sectional interests set themselves the target of preserving the full range of differentials on the higher base of the guaranteed minimum income, the resulting inflationary pressure added to the other pressures could destroy the opportunity of steady and sustained growth which independence will offer.

The danger of intense sectional competition for resources in an expanding Scottish economy will be increased by the greater proportionate power which employee organisations are likely to enjoy in Scotland. Given the dominant role of the state, it is likely that an even higher proportion of the Scottish labour force than at present will be employed in the public sector (currently about 33% of the Scottish labour force compared to about 30% in the United Kingdom as a whole), where market discipline is non-existent and where, as a result, employee militancy, particularly among the higher paid sections, has recently been on the increase.

A Scottish government's greatest asset in facing these problems will be its ability to offer a credible prospect of rising real standards of living. Its second most important asset will be the fear of the destruction of that prospect. But these intangible assets have to be turned into specific policies, and no technical economic or institutional device can protect a democratic government from sectional or popular pressure to pursue misguided economic policies. Workers' control will certainly put the responsibility for decision-taking in the given circumstances on the employees. But the government can change circumstances — or at least some of them — and the public can change the government.

The success of offering tax reductions or increases in the social wage in return for union support for an incomes' policy will depend on the unions' own assessment of the opportunities for advancing their sectional interest which they will sacrifice by acceptance. The government could certainly include in its package an offer of action to reduce the grosser inequalities of wealth. But, regrettably, this demand has not been high on the unions' shopping list in their recent bargaining with the London Government.

It is probable that observed differences of income generate more resentment, insecurity and competitiveness among sectional groups than veiled differences of wealth. And in their post-socialist manifestation, the success of organised sectional groups, and above all of their professional leadership, is measured precisely by the spirit of competitiveness they display in defending, or improving, their position on the incomes' ladder. Social democracy, born from a universalist inspiration out of the needs of one broad, majority interest, seems now to be tied to a Procrustean bed of competing sectional interests.

Scottish Radical Democracy

Radical measures of economic equalisation may have to wait on the outcome of efforts to inculcate in the competing interests a new sense of community and democratic responsibility. While an independent Scotland is unlikely to prove more sympathetic than other industrialised societies to efforts to restore a traditional *communitas,* independence will offer an opportunity of testing the strength of the radical aspirations which support the myth of Scottish Democracy.

Among the elements of a revived Scottish democracy should be a Bill of Rights embracing, among the familiar individual, religious and political rights, a Freedom of Press Act on the Swedish model: the introduction of proportional representation: provision for referenda, including initiative referenda: a radical decentralisation of power within Scotland to all-purpose local authorities possessing a wider and more elastic tax base than is afforded by the present rating system, as well as powers of industrial initiative: the development of a system of specialist committees in the Scottish legislature: the broadcasting of the Scottish Parliament: measures facilitating the creation of new Scottish-based newspapers and journals organised on workers' control principles: public participation in the control of broadcasting media, perhaps through some version of the Dutch Television Foundation: and the establishment of a system of Neighbourhood Law Centres, with salaried staff, to extend the individual's ability to enjoy his statutory rights.

These political reform complementing the measures of decentralisation and democratisation in the industrial field, would provide the institutional framework for a democratic Scottish society.

The priority in the educational field should be the extension of the comprehensive principle to post-school education, replacing the present system which reserves higher education to a selected minority usually at one period of their lives, with a system designed to give the citizen non-selective access to further and higher education in the form of accumulated entitlements to day and period release and sabbaticals, throughout his life. The extension of educational provision in this way would help to lift the incubus of examinations from Scottish schools and give substance to the alluring vision of Scotland as an educated democracy, the true home of the democratic intellect.

In the social field a nationwide network of paid, part-time, neighbourhood social workers should be established to act as a community-based source of help and channel of liaison with the professional social work services. This would provide a local complement to the national strategy for welfare based on a guaranteed minimum income and on environmental improvement.

A programme of radical democracy in political institutions, industry, welfare and education is consistent with the generic definition of social democracy as the pursuit of social justice in a liberal framework. But it directly challenges today's received social democratic orthodoxy — which too easily accepts the centralisation of power even to the point of legitimising the corporate state; which supports a mixed economy even when the mix is increasingly one between centralised state and private corporations; which has made a dogma out of rationalisation and integration; which has tolerated large scale poverty in the midst of affluence in the complacent hope that economic growth would open the way to a politically painless redistribution of wealth; which has failed to seek new forms of democratic community to moderate the rivalries of competing sectional interests; and which has allowed a concept of politics as a manipulative exercise undertaken to create and maintain a compliant consensus to smother the radical ideal of politics as a central activity in a socially responsible and vigorously self-critical culture.

The dogmatic political realist will of course discount this vision of a radical alternative to social democracy against its lack of any strong interest group support. In so doing, he runs the risk of underestimating the extent to which nationalism — by publicising old ideals and proclaiming new standards, by accelerating the rate of social and economic change and by uniting different sectional groups behind a common aim — can open up new political perspectives.

The historical sources of radicalism in Scotland are diverse, not to say disparate. Although the claim that class division is a wicked English import must be dismissed, the ethos of Scottish society is more egalitarian than that of English society. This egalitarianism, in part the legacy of Calvinist radicalism, in part of a romantic and selective retrospect of Scottish history, has survived the decline in the national role of the Protestant churches and the universities which once gave it institutional expression, albeit incomplete. The legend of Red Clydeside, and the popular myth — which owes more to the idosyncracies of the British electoral system than to anything else — that Scotland is a socialist country — may perhaps be taken as testifying to an unsatisfied political idealism.

More substantial is the radical tradition in Scottish politics, which found expression through the Liberal Party in the nineteenth century, then, as the industrial crisis deepened and the influence of religion waned, through the Labour Party, and is now finding expression, as the British idea declines, through the Scottish National Party. Consistent with that tradition there is among many Scottish intellectuals a gratifying suspicion of the doctrine of Parliamentary sovereignty as an alien and stultifying dogma, and an acceptance of the politically more suggestive doctrine of popular sovereignty, claimed as a distinctive theme in Scottish history.

The contemporary sources of radicalism are no less disparate. The circumstances facing an independent Scotland will, it has been argued, dictate an economic radicalism which will not easily be contained within the bounds of conventional social democracy. The rhetoric of the Nationalist movement will have created high expectations of social reform in an independent Scotland. As a genuine nationalism (cf. John Mackintosh and others who persist in seeing Scotland as a "quasi-nation" presumably incapable of nurturing a mature nationalism) the independence movement is likely to demonstrate a specific hostility to the integrationist and federalist aims of most social democrats. As Scotland's cultural, linguistic and regional complexity enhances the movement's role as a vehicle for the general reaction against over-centralisation, so Scotland's inherited sense of being "agin the Government" adds strength to the reaction against bureaucratic, "closed" government.

The post-Imperial rediscovery of Scotland's identity as a small European nation has produced a welcome readiness to seek in the experience of other small democratic countries — particularly Norway — political, social and economic lessons for Scotland, while the discovery of Scotland's wealth of energy resources at a time of near panic about future supplies of all basic resources, has reinforced a concern for man's relationship with his environment and for a proper balance between population and resources which was first stimulated among Scottish intellectuals in the mid-war period as they assessed Scotland's experience of industrialisation.

Whatever its historical role the social democracy preached today in the

United Kingdom represents a stale conventional wisdom which too often serves as an apology for conservatism. In the approach to independence, the S.N.P. must strive to synthesise disparate pressures and ideals into an alternative programme of radical democracy.

1 The *Scotsman* — 6th December 1974.
2 Anthony Crosland — "Social Democracy in Europe", p 3. Fabian Tract no. 438.
3 Ibid. p 11.
4 Ibid. p 2.
5 N. Bosanquet: p 17, "The Real Low Pay Problem" in "Low Pay", edited by Frank Field, Arrow Books. 1973.
6 P 170, "Poverty in Dortmund", (Poverty Report). Temple Smith. 1975.
7 S. Ringen — "Welfare Studies in Scandinavia", Scandinavian Political Studies, Vol. 9. 1974.
8 Roy Jenkins — *The Listener*, 12th February 1976.
9 George Reid — *New Outlook*, February 1976.
10 S.N.P. Industrial Development Policy. Agenda of Annual Conference 1976.
11 John Firn: p 158. "External Control and Regional Policy", in "Red Paper on Scotland", Edinburgh University Students' Publication Board, 1975.
12 Roy Jenkins: op. cit.
13 Cf. J. E. Meade: p 46, "The Intelligent Radical's Guide to the Mixed Economy", Allen and Unwin. 1975.
14 See "Industrial Democracy and Social Ownership", Co-operative Party. 1974.
15 Peter Jay: "Inflation, Employment and Politics". Occasional Paper 46. Institute of Economic Affairs. 1976.
16 S.N.P. Press Statement, George Reid M.P., 24th April 1974.
17 Ian Levitt, footnote 1, p 332. "Poverty in Scotland" in "Red Paper on Scotland", E.U.S.P.B. 1975.
18 Samuel Brittan, p 202 seq. "Capitalism and the Permissive Society". Macmillan. 1973.
19 Royal Commission on the Distribution of Income and Wealth Report No. 3. P 31, Higher Incomes from Employment. H.M.S.O. Cmnd. 6383.
20 Royal Commission on the Distribution of Income and Wealth, p 123. Report No. 1. Initial report on standing reference. H.M.S.O. Cmnd. 6171.

NATIONALISM, COMMUNITY AND DEMOCRACY

Isobel Lindsay

One of the most striking things about the conventional political debate is what it has not been about. Many of the fundamental developments in our society have gone almost without comment by mainstream politicians of right or left. Our only legacy has been a sterile, highly ritualised debate about the marginal redistribution of the spoils. There has been an almost total failure to come to terms with the social and political problems generated by the development of highly centralised, advanced industrial societies whether of East or West or to question the purposes and limitations of economic growth. The development of the nationalist movement in Scotland and elsewhere is not a quaint aberration or a simple campaign for economic betterment; it is concerned with how a modern society can fulfill the social, emotional and material needs of its citizens.

One of the problems we face is that the language of politics is so inadequate. The conventional political language and the old ideologies have not kept pace with what is happening in our societies and this is far from being a matter of mere academic interest. The actions we take are largely determined by how we see the problem but our insight is structured by the prevalent terminology. This has a powerful circular effect — because political language is inadequate, people find it hard to verbalise about things which may be very important to them and consequently political leaders get the feedback they expect expressed in the language with which they are entirely familiar. Doing research in industry, I found it not uncommon to get comments like — "They used to know who you were in here but now we're just cogs in a wheel" — but I would be amazed if any employee ever raised this point at a union meeting or with their M.P. The problem in contemporary politics is not just that there has been a failure to find the right answers; much more damning has been the failure even to ask the right questions. There are so many areas of life in which politicians have not talked about the possible options because they genuinely thought that there were no viable choices other than the *status quo* or because they simply did not think. Consequently the public were not stimulated into awareness of the different directions in which society might develop.

The reaction to the nationalist parties in Scotland and Wales has been characterised more than anything else by resentment and incomprehension because we have introduced a new dimension (literal as well as metaphorical) for which no provision has been made in established political thinking. The threat that we pose is not just a threat to seats, it is a threat to fixed ideas, to long-established certainties. This is the most unforgiveable political sin of all.

Nationalism

The debate on Scottish independence has been clouded by the confused thinking which surrounds the concept of nationalism. It is often regarded as something which must be either morally good or morally bad in itself rather than something which, in its broadest sense of attachment to a territorial and/or cultural community, is morally neutral. To define nationalism in abstract as either good or bad is rather like saying that the sex drive in abstract is good or bad whether it be rape or between consenting adults. The sentiments which attach people to place and to kin are of fundamental importance to any highly socialised animal with a complex culture. This attachment serves two purposes. It helps to create an overriding loyalty to balance the inevitable conflicts and tensions which will arise when people live in proximity to each other. More important, even the simplest culture cannot survive without continuity and stability. If, to reduce it to absurdity, we had no particular territorial or group attachments and we all led an individualistic, nomadic existence, it would be virtually impossible to pass on knowledge and values in any systematic way. Therefore, whether you call it tribalism, nationalism, patriotism, this sentiment is not atavistic. Its absence in a modern society is not a sign of emancipation. It is, on the contrary, quite fundamental to what we are.

Having said that nationalism *per se* is a morally neutral concept, one must point out that there is an important and valid distinction between nationalism and imperialism although the former can degenerate into the latter. Attachment to one's own community in no way implies any desire or necessity to deprive others of similar rights. It is, in fact, quite in keeping with a preparedness to defend the rights of others to self-determination within their own territory. Imperialism, on the other hand, arises from the desire of one territorial or ideological group to impose its will on another. It may be done in the name of nationalism, religion, capitalism, socialism or whatever but it does not follow that nationalism, religion, capitalism or socialism must of themselves be imperialist.

Nationalism is neither geographically nor culturally static. Changing circumstances may forge new identities and new groupings although the emotional need for continuity and stability is likely to ensure that attachments do not change rapidly. Nationalism can also at different times and in different situations be a centralising or a decentralising force. For example, in the United States "nationalism" is associated with the Federal Government as opposed to State or lower level community political power. In this century, however, nationalism has probably been more significant as a decentralising force, most notably in the case of the nationalist movements breaking down the former centralised imperialist empires and, of course, what we now see emerging is the growth of decentralising nationalism or regionalism in the highly developed industrialised societies. These centralised advanced societies are beginning to face an internal challenge and it is groups with a long-established political/cultural identity which are spear-heading this challenge. The problems which give rise to it, however, have wider relevance and the success of the more culturally distinctive areas may very well stimulate others.

It is interesting to contrast what have been the central concerns of the social sciences and those of the politicians. It may, of course, be plausible to dismiss the pre-occupation with such faddish ideas as alienation and anomie as merely the products of intellectuals with problems but perhaps we can credit them with some degree of imaginative insight into the human condition. So many of the themes which have, for example, dominated sociology have largely been accepted in conventional politics as "given" factors not open to real change through the political process. I would like to look at three of these central ideas — culture, community and power.

Culture

Perhaps the most central of all is the concept of "culture" — the intricate, complex, pervasive and distinctive way in which societies have evolved and individuals are socialised into them and take identity and meaning from them. It was fashionable not so very many years ago deliberately to destroy established cultures for the sake of "emancipation" or creed or greed. It is still being done but it has become less fashionable to proclaim it. The plight of many of the indigenous peoples of North and South America, of Africa, of Australasia has become the subject of sympathetic media treatment. These show in extreme form the demoralisation, the disorientation, the loss of personal identity which results. But those who readily condemn the dramatic examples are often remarkably slow to draw any lessons of relevance to our own society. Of course, we do not have such extreme cases (although the Gaelic-speaking communities could offer many examples from the not too distant past) but the same processes have been in operation. This is the point that Pier Paule Paselinni was trying to make in the context of Italian society — the rapid destruction of an older social network, the loss of community, the imposition of different values.

If there is something of a class stereotype in the attitudes of the Scots to the English, then it is because the Scots as a nation — middle as well as working class — have experienced something akin to what the lower classes experience as a sub-group in the larger society. Our language or dialect was rejected as inferior and the centres of power and influence increasingly moved outwith the country. With the growth of centralised media the people who dominated entertainment and current affairs were certainly not Scots. If you wanted to be considered really successful you had to go South, if you wanted to get something done, all too often you had to go cap in hand to London. Scotland was the poor relation, the dependent, the small and weak partner. The cumulative effect of this has been to produce in the Scots and sense of being, in Norman McCaig's words, "a failed nation".

It is, of course, twentieth century developments which more than any other period have produced this effect. The cultural impact of the loss of political independence was comparatively slight in earlier periods when the role of central government was a very limited one, when economic activity was more localised in control and communications not highly centralised. But to lack political independence in the modern situation has a much more important cultural impact. It not only deprives us of a powerful tool of protection and reform which can be used to counteract economic and cultural centralism, it also deprives us of the political expression of national identity and in that sense is a dimunition of the latter.

Ultimately it is hard to envisage a situation in which a high degree of political and/or cultural centralism will not have a debilitating effect on the peripheries. The vicarious identification with a more dominant culture may carry with it a heavy social cost.

This problem of culture and cultural change is one which ought, theoretically, to be of some interest to Conservatives but in theory and practice they have shown a gross insensitivity to it. They have been the supporters of rampant commercialism, they have been on the frontline of those who chide workers for not migrating around the country to get any available job, they have never hesitated to support development whatever the social cost. Their reaction to oil developments has been an excellent example of this. The S.N.P. argued that for local community reasons as well as resource conservation, oil developments should not be pushed too rapidly. The only people who opposed this position perhaps more vehemently than the oil companies were the Conservatives. Apart from the Nationalists there is no major political party for whom the issues of culture and cultural change are of real importance.

Power

If there is one factor which exposes the total inadequacies of mainstream Socialist and Conservative thinking, it is their failure to come to terms with the problems of power in contemporary society. On the socialist side we still have the Marxist legacy, excusable in Marx given the particular circumstances of his own time, of assuming private legal ownership to be synonymous with power and further assuming that the transfer from private legal ownership to public legal ownership will, of itself, constitute major social change. Max Weber at the beginning of the century aptly predicted "For the time being the dictatorship of the official and not that of the worker is on the march".

If you try to redefine the class struggle in terms of the distribution of power rather than the legal relationship to property (and what is property if not simply one form of power), as Ralf Dahrendorf did in his book *Class and Class Conflict in an Industrial Society,* you produce a model in many respects more applicable to our own society and certainly one which can more readily explain the centre/periphery conflict.

One of the other faults in the discussion of class conflict by the mainstream left is the assumption that conflict in society is at root one-dimensional, that it is really about the wealthy and the poor and that other conflicts are simply confusions, digressions, "false consciousness". And yet if you look, say, at the planning decisions in our cities which have had such a major effect on people's lives, is this simply to do with the relationship between the rich and the poor? If you look at the problems which arise in most industries, will there ever not be real conflicts about the pace of change, about differentials, about the right of some people to tell others what to do irrespective of whether the industry is privately or publicly owned? Of course the relative distribution of wealth and the degree of power derived from private wealth will be a major issue in most societies but if it is to be understood, it must be seen in the total context of social conflict not as a unique factor which in some sense causes everything else.

Within the traditions of British socialism there was a strand more conscious of these other dimensions. Romantic socialists like William Morris and Guild Socialists like G. D. H. Cole, were most concerned with the problems of community and culture and centralised power — in Cole's phrase the problems of "democracy face to face with hugeness". But this attempt to develop a "community" socialism was totally swamped in the face of conventional statism. If you believe that the object of radical politics is to ensure the delivery of a comparable quantity of goods to the citizens of a state, then it may be that the crude, centralised statist solution has something to commend it although in reality the distribution of goods too often goes hand in hand with the distribution of power and prestige, whatever the formal aims of public policy. However, if you feel that in working towards a more egalitarian society the distribution of power and status must stand along with the distribution of goods as of central importance in political policy, then the solutions must be decentralising ones. Whatever the large centralised state can achieve in terms of redistribution of wealth (probably not very much), it is almost impossible by definition that it can fulfill any major power and status redistribution unless it destroys itself. At best it may change the nature of the elite groups. To achieve this more fundamental egalitarianism you must radically disperse the points of power and initiative and communication in society.

Little reference has been made to the Conservative position because, in modern U.K. politics, Conservatives have made so little attempt to think out any consistent position at all. Interestingly, unlike their counter-parts in some other countries, British Conservatives have not at all been critical of big business nor have they been notably the champions of local or regional "rights" against the centre. Their rhetoric has been heavily weighted with attacks on state power although their actions in office have belied this. Their philosophical base has been shoddy and inconsistent; growing centralisation in the private sector is not criticised and their policy priority appears to be that of transferring a few powers from the powerful public sector to the powerful/privileged private sector. Many American conservatives are critical of big business as well as big government. It is not moving power sideways that matters most; it is in reducing the size of the political units that the best hope of social and political democratisation now lies.

Community

"Where power is external or centralised, where it relieves groups of persons of the trouble of making important decisions, where it is penetrating and minute, then, no matter how wise and good it may be in principle, it is difficult for a true community to develop. Community thrives on self-help (and a little disorder), either corporate or individual, and everything that removes a group from the performance of, or involvement in, its own government can hardly help but weaken the sense of community." (Robert Nisbet).

We use the word community in two senses — to indicate a geographical area with interacting social institutions and in the other subjective usage, a feeling of belonging, a sense of special identification with a particular grouping of people. Both are of great importance; both have been substantially ignored as matters of political interest. The size and the shape of our communities has major economic and social implications and Scotland has just about the worst of all worlds in its (expensive) extremes of rural depopulation and urban congestion. In city redevelopment we have created huge, unpopular, aesthetically unattractive, single-class ghettoes and most of it "just happened". We still find politicians discussing problems of crime and punishment as if these could be divorced from the nature of the community, from the weakening of one of the most powerful controlling factors of all — knowing and being known.

Human beings will normally seek "community" in its subjective sense. The point at issue is not whether they will seek it but in what form will they seek it and whether they will achieve it. The quotation from Nisbet brings out a most valuable point about the inter-relationship of democracy and community. Political decision-making in its broadest sense provides a socially creative channel through which people can work out their priorities, their values, their goals and they can act in some respects as a collectivity. A political unit can provide a goal for collective achievement, something which has greater continuity through time than any individual. It may reinforce community at the same time as requiring community to provide its coherence.

The question of the basis on which political units should be determined must ultimately rest on value judgments. If you believe that people should be participants rather than voyeurs, that variety is an important factor in stimulating creativity, then you will favour trying to keep as much decision-making as possible close to those whom it will most effect. But the other factor with which you must work is that political units should where possible reflect community identifications and this may be determined by historical experience, by cultural differences, by differing interests. It is remarkable that the feeling of being Scottish should have remained. We ought to have become North British but being awkward and unreasonable, we didn't. For the people who live in Scotland, Scotland is a meaningful aggregate and we want to achieve the political expression of this national identity. We are even bold enough to think that we might make not such a bad job of it as our present masters. What the ultimate pattern of decision-making within Scotland will be is a choice for the post-independence situation but the thinking which leads to self-government is likely to be the thinking which will lead to a vigorous local and industrial democracy.

Scottish nationalism is open-ended; it is a beginning not a conclusion.

COMMUNAL IDENTITY IN ORKNEY
AND SHETLAND

Howie Firth

Orcadians and Shetlanders are very tolerant people, yet there is a line that no man should cross. A distant government did so in the late'sixties, decreeing that the islands' water supplies should be administered from much further south, as part of a massive new Highland regional unit. The resulting fight not only eventually won back separate water boards, but ensured that Orkney and Shetland came out of the post-Wheatley local government reorganisation with separate autonomous Islands Councils.

One clue to the strength of island reaction comes from a statement made by the Presbytery of Orkney at the height of the storm. The Government, they said, were "destroying the soul of Orkney". Today, without such an obvious external enemy, the problem of communal identity remains.

Oppression in the Past

Orkney had many reasons to be unafraid of oil; more than a few outwardly catastrophic events had given the islands long-term material benefits. The Napoleonic Wars diverted shipping from the closed Channel ports to Kirkwall and Stromness, to the benefit of local merchants, while the wartime demand for iodine sent the price of Orcadian kelp soaring. In the present century, two world wars left Orkney with a number of roads, airports, piers, even the Churchill barriers, not to mention fresh capital.

Shetland, by contrast, could look back with some bitterness on its contacts with the south. The Napoleonic Wars, and many years of colonial wars before, brought the pressgang in search of sea-going Shetlanders. By the time of Trafalgar, there were no less than 3,000 Shetlanders forced into the Royal Navy, from a community with a population of 22,000.

Worst of all were the oppressions of the Scottish lairds of the eighteenth and nineteenth centuries.

Shetland's rich fishing grounds had led to close economic ties with Germany and The Netherlands; but the French almost destroyed the Dutch herring fleet in 1703, and the restrictions on salt for curing fish which followed the Act of Union killed off the trade of the German merchants. It left the Scottish lairds in complete control of every aspect of Shetland life, land and economy, and the bitter memories of oppression still remain.

Thus Shetland's reaction to oil development was to seek from central government the strongest powers they could get, to argue from strength against the incoming oil companies. The Shetlanders could point out with justification that they did not need oil; that the Shetland economy had at last begun to boom, as capital from government agencies like the White Fish Authority and the Highland Board had become available to enable the carefully made plans of the fishing and knitwear industries to be turned into reality.

Impact of the Oil

The Zetland County Council Act of 1974 gave the council more power than any other local authority in the U.K. It could be seen on the one hand as the power to allow oil developments to proceed smoothly; on the other as the power to protect the Shetland people from the worst of the consequences of oil, and to enable them to share some of the benefits.

Shetland Islands Council is now a partner in the £100 million construction of Europe's largest oil terminal, at Sullum Voe. It was able to tell the oil companies to build a pier at Calback, so that all materials for site work were landed by sea there; and then to charge 1p for every gross registered ton of shipping that used the pier.

It was also able to refuse Shell a licence for the Brent Field pipeline until the company had trawled up every piece of debris from the seabed along the path of the pipe.

Orkney, by contrast, looked forward to oil as the opportunity to diversify. The basic industry of agriculture had become highly mechanised, and thus employment dropped, despite the signs of success evident in the appearance of new silos and farm steadings and the reclaimed acres of hill ground which were added to the existing mass of rich green fields. For Orkney, the oil invasion would bring employment, people, houses and capital, like several other invasions before.

Two years after, despite an undoubted increase in prosperity, a rather gloomy view prevailed of Orkney Islands Council's oil powers, which, although rather watered down from Shetland's precedent, were still substantial. The islanders of Flotta had seen the building of the terminal for the Piper and Claymore oilfields cause them to spend two years wading through a sea of mud. Thirty-ton lorries had destroyed much of their roads into a mass of potholes, mud and boulders. Their pier, when they could use it, was frequently under several inches of water, and the council had neither appointed a piermaster to supervise it nor even, apparently, sent anyone out to collect harbour dues. To some, it was almost as if a circle had been drawn round the island, and the laws of normal life put into indefinite suspension within it.

Crisis in Identity

In the midst of the oil boom, the problem of identity came to the surface in a rather unexpected way. It was not the raw reality of the industry's presence in daily life, which many people had for better or worse taken for granted for the moment. This time the question had been asked in the London papers: would Scottish independence send Orkney and Shetland on their own way, even to join Norway?

The question never became one of serious political debate, but it did lead to the deeper one of identity. Had we really been Vikings all the time, were we even still, as one enthusiast put it, "the Norse people of the sagas"? It could be argued that there was a pattern of Norse settlement from about A.D. 800 until the annexation by Scotland in 1468. There were Norse farm names, family names, dialect words, documents in Norse still appearing in Orkney in the fifteenth century, and in Shetland till the seventeenth century.

But after the night-out in Viking costume, the next day brings a twentieth century hangover. If there were Vikings, did they survive the dark years under the lairds, or did they go away, to build up the Greenland and Antarctic whaling fisheries, the Hudson's Bay Company, the frontiers of the British Empire? In 1799 almost four out of five men in the Hudson's Bay Company were Orcadian. Also a Prime Minister of New Zealand (Robert Stout) and the founder of the P. & O. (Arthur Anderson) were Shetlanders.

The solution to the problem of identity is more complex than a mere donning of fourteenth century Norwegian clothes. The threads must include the dedication and skill of the people who aligned the Standing Stones at Brogar with unerring accuracy to predict the eclipses of the moon; the persistence and doggedness of the crofters and fishermen who survived decades of oppression and near starvation; the adaptability and practicality of people who could survive on rocks like the Out Skerries, cutting seaweed by hand to fertilise the scanty pockets of soil, or build up farms, ranches, companies, even empires thousands of miles away from home.

The next crisis in the struggle of identity may come, not in Shetland but in Orkney, where the Island Council have done something that few outside bodies would have dared, and which strikes deep at the roots of every Orcadian. In islands which are abundant in ideal building land, they have imposed a rigid "green belt" policy on the people, sterilising whole stretches of "unspoiled" countryside from house-building. Private house-building is virtually frozen in a wide zone around Kirkwall, and the consequence is rocketing inflation in prices of building land. For the first time ever, Orcadians have been forced to ask the question: is the countryside a living and developing part of our lives, or is it merely a museum-place for tourists or a tranquilliser for jaded townspeople?

In Shetland the problem of identity is subtler, but just as deep. The skill of the council in heading off the first anticipated threats of oil development, along with the sheer force of the boom, seemed at first to take the strength away from any potentital public debate.

Yet now, there are signs of more restlessness. A feeling is growing that there should be more public participation, that the council's contact with the public should go deeper into the grass roots.

Need for Participation

At the end of last December the editor of the *Shetland Times* expressed his unease at the dearth of debate of where Shetland was heading. We are making progress, he said, but progress to what? What would happen to local employment when the oil construction boom was over? How should the oil revenues be used to strengthen the Shetland economy? What training should be developed for the young men who had flocked to unskilled but highly paid jobs? And what were the real features of the "Shetland way of life".

More recently, Councillor Edward Thomason, a former county convener, asked the Council's Policy Committee to review its procedures, asking for a freer and more wide ranging discussion on ideas in the council. The sheer volume of work coming before the council had led to a situation where so much had to be processed by the council's management team, and Councillor Thomason felt that he had become "a member of a decision-taking body rather than a deliberative body".

The *Shetland Times* editorial seemed to put its finger on what was happening: "One cannot but feel for councillors who, elected as parish representatives, often to deal merely with parish-pump problems, now find themselves responsible for political discussion, often of national as well as local importance. . . . Now it is possible to shift into a higher gear; to keep pace with events we all have to."

The higher gear must involve wider public participation. It is hard for people outside Orkney and Shetland to realise what a narrow pool the new island councillors were drawn from. In a one-tier authority all employees were excluded from standing for the council: no teachers, council office workers, manual and supervisory staff. Employment considerations forced many others — small farmers, shopkeepers — to stand down. The result is that about half Shetland's councillors are over 65, while Orkney's tend to come from a prosperous middle class, most owning substantial homes.

Somehow the pool must be widened, to leaven the undoubted experience of the older generation with the technical skills and ambition of the young who will have to live with the consequences of the council's decisions. Either full-time councillors or a different pattern of meetings and expenses must be tried.

It also strains council's time and small communities' patience, when every single decision of every parish and island has to be channelled through council meetings, at which they have at most one representative.

The lack of participation is felt in the outer islands and parishes, who at present do not even have the sop of a Community Council to give them the illusion of involvement. Consultation is not enough; actual statutory power must be devolved to district councils, with resources to maintain and build roads, piers and even factories.

At the same time, with the councils possessing such wide powers, including the power to invest in companies, and several million pounds of oil "disturbance" money, there is scope for asking some deeper, long-term questions about the Orkney and Shetland economies than before.

Economic Problems

Too often Orkney and Shetland export raw materials and import the finished product. One consequence is a dependence on the vicissitudes of market prices.

In 1967, the English wool market collapsed and the Shetland crofters' return fell. By contrast, when the Japanese bought up wool heavily, the Shetland knitters had to pay an inflated price for wool.

Similarly, Orkney farming is geared to producing a massive output of store cattle to be shipped south during a few weeks in autumn. The price that the farmer gets is affected by the conditions of the Aberdeen market and the success of the operation depends on the shipping running smoothly.

On the other hand, the islands depend heavily on the steady flow of imports from mainland Scotland. After a week's strike at Aberdeen docks in October 1975, Shetland shops had virtually run out of eggs, butter, bacon, yeast and frozen foods. Recently Mr Prophet Smith of the H.I.D.B. recalled that when he left Shetland 16 years ago, they did not import milk. Now some 3,000 gallons are shipped in every week from Aberdeen.

A recent letter in the *Shetland Times* pointed out that "not so long ago Shetland supported over 30,000 people, or rather, they supported themselves. Now the lack of one boatload of food leads to a minor crisis after less than a week, and it is not difficult to imagine conditions which would lead to serious shortage and some hardship on the islands".

One lesson in diversification comes from the Shetland fishing industry. By developing local fish-processing the industry has products that can be marketed in a variety of places and ways, to give the best return.

An analogous solution for the Shetland knitting industry might be a Shetland spinning mill. The industry would then no longer be fragmented, but involve Shetland control in grading and storing the clip, spinning it, knitting Shetland patterns and selling the finished knitwear as a high-quality product with a trademark, emphasising the strength and quality of the native wool.

The next stage for Orcadian agriculture involves a slaughterhouse to E.E.C. standards, able to ship sides of prime quality Orkney beef to any market where the price is right. Instead of depending on market prices for a satisfactory return there is the option to hold back the product until the price rises, with the E.E.C. intervention price to fall back on.

The role here of the new councils is crucial, for in their oil revenues there is a readily mobilised source of capital for such enterprises. Even these funds may not be sufficient, however; Shetland's fishing industry will need massive capital expenditure to provide new piers and breakwaters, and there will be many competing schemes all deserving cash.

Now there is at present a massive cash inflow in the islands. In one sense there has always been surplus cash for investment. For instance, Orkney puts £3 million into national savings each year and Shetland is not far behind. National banks and building societies have played a major part in the economic life of the islands. But there are now immense additional sums of money moving around Orkney and Shetland and the waters of the North Sea.

The problem is not cash *inflow*: it is cash *availability*. All the cash now flowing in and around the islands will slip away like sand through the fingers unless it can be channelled into local industries by a local island bank. With a U.K. recession, money is too expensive to borrow and the advantage goes to the big company with money of its own to invest. Yet with the present oil boom in Orkney and Shetland, now is the time for local people to invest in developing new industries and expanding old ones.

Long-term questions have to be asked about transport. Up till now, the islands have been mainly concerned with the soaring costs of their links with Thurso and Aberdeen. The transport pattern has developed whereby Orkney and Shetland are each a "hinterland" of a centre on mainland Scotland.

Yet it must be asked if it makes economic sense for Orkney store cattle to be shipped to Aberdeen, fattened and killed there, and the resultant beef to be shipped to Shetland. With Shetland importing food heavily, the economies of both island groups would be strengthened by establishing an efficient shipping link between the two, rather than send so much through Aberdeen.

A further question that must be asked is the role in the islands of education in its present form. For long it has emphasised the pupil who wants to "get on" and gain entrance qualifications for an academic life elsewhere.

The system may have to modify its aims in an era of rapid local development and demand for skilled labour (including skilled thinkers). The ultimate aim of the islands should be something more than the simple export of store cattle and professors.

Public Accountability

As for the links with central government, let them be obvious and clear-cut. Shetland has already shown it can devise layouts for housing schemes far better on its own than when it has to follow formulae for packing so many people to the acre. Orkney has shown that it is highly susceptible to any hints or guidelines from Edinburgh, which it is liable to grasp like Moses when offered the tablets of stone. It is much safer to let Orkney Council develop its own housing ideas in a dialogue with the Orkney people.

The key concept must be that of accountability. The present system of rate support grant whereby "the government" pays so many pounds on approved projects for every one spent locally is outworn. It encourages occasional squandering, prevents the determination of priorities, and gives a slow and inflexible response to problems of rapid growth and corresponding demand for infrastructure. A new system is required where the councils raise their money locally, determine how to spend it, and are accountable to the public for their actions. (And if that doesn't stimulate public participation, nothing will.)

One system of local income tax could be operated in conjunction with central government via the computer at East Kilbride. Under this system, rapid growth leading to a demand for increased infrastructure will thereby also produce the higher quantities of revenue necessary to finance it.

Shortfall should certainly come from a fixed percentage of oil revenues, but additional possibilities include motor vehicle tax and even, in Shetland's case, customs duties.

A pointer to the direction that events are now converging in came from S.N.P. conference resolutions in 1968 and 1970. Following earlier S.N.P. support for Orkney and Shetland's struggle against enforced local government amalgamation, the resolutions sought to build island autonomy into the constitution of a self-governing Scotland. The successful examples of Faroe and the Isle of Man were quoted.

Today in the north we are no longer content merely with occasional reaction against central government or abstract discussion of "Faroese status". We are concerned with nothing less than the actual identity of our community, both with what we are and where we are going.

In the flux of events involving North Sea oil development and the break up of the old imperial centre at Westminster, the problems of communal identity are again emerging in the islands of the north.

THE HIGHLAND "PROBLEM"

Andrew Currie

To the casual observer, it might appear that the entire production of timber from Highland forests each year cannot keep pace with the consumption of wood pulp in publications about the Highlands and Islands. Though ample in quantity these publications disseminate little relevant information about the region. They are largely of a unique literary genre, apparently written by the totally ill-informed, or perhaps by the cynical and, wrapped in tartans of dubious authenticity, they are consumed by a world-wide readership of armchair tourists who must surely be oblivious to the absurdity of the view of the Highlands and Islands they contain. A small number contain serious and superficially reasonable contributions to the "solution of the Highland 'Problem' " but very few of these adequatley examine the very nature of the "Problem" itself.

The Highlands and Islands are commonly felt to be an "underdeveloped" area, and it is widely believed that if only suitable light industry could be attracted to communities throughout the region, incomes would rise, emigration would cease and all would live happily ever after. Others, however, think in more grandiose terms and seek salvation in massive petro-chemical projects (and in soaring property values) or think fashionably small and visualise a landscape of traditional black houses (with suitable mod. cons. installed) in which a population of craftsman/philosphers manufacture authentic craft goods for sale to an unending stream of "up-market" visitors passing their doors. Others again, perhaps more cynical, ascribe the current "underdevelopment" of the Highlands to the intrinsic laziness of its people who are alleged to finance, by government subsidy or spasmodic employment on public works, a life of over-indulgence in strong liquor or stronger religion or possibly both. To all these schools of thought, "underdevelopment" is an implicit, and unquestioned root cause of the Highland "Problem".

An equally commonly held set of assumptions is the view that the region is totally dependent on outside assistance in the form of both operating subsidies and capital investment, especially in transport, and that central government has a moral obligation to provide such facilities. This view is particularly strongly supported by people living outside the Highlands. The well-disposed Lowlander will offer the Government's cheque book as soon as the Highland "Problem" is mentioned, promising free ferries, motorways to Inverness and a network of sea, plane or hovercraft services. Even in the Highlands, where there is noticeably more common sense on the subject, political reputations can be made leading campaigns to span unfrequented firths with multi-million pound dreams of concrete and steel; no-one gets too excited by the subsidised and infrequent bus, timetabled to leave five minutes before the subsidised and even less frequent train is due to arrive. Few even begin to ask whether the Highlands and Islands might not be economically viable if the regional economy was managed with the interest of the region paramount and not merely exploited for the benefit of organisations and individuals who make no real attempt to identify with the indigenous communities.

Romantics and Modernists

A realistic prescription for the Highlands can only follow an accurate prognosis of the region's current condition and this is bedevilled by the confused and often contradictory perceptions of the situation and of how it has arisen. Confusion and contradiction are no monopoly of the outside observer as the ambivalent behaviour of many Highland communities clearly demonstrates: a private and negative contempt for the laird or the insensitive incomer is too often expressed in public deference and apathetic collaboration. Within this mixture of conflicting and incoherent perceptions two outlooks are prominent which might usefully be labelled as the Romantic and the Modernist.

The Romantic view extols co-operation but is fundamentally paternalistic, constantly harks back to the Forty-Five and the Clearances without grasping the contemporary significance of either, and advocates crofting and craft industry as if both were somehow survivors from an earlier golden age.

The Modernist, on the other hand, urges the virtues of competition whilst working to achieve a self-interested monopoly, and demands a belated participation in the agricultural and industrial revolutions.

Although apparently mutually contradictory, both views are based on similar, and mistaken, views of the history of the Highlands and Islands, for the region today, even its crofting and craft industry, is the product of the economic transformation which is said to have passed the area by.

Highlands in History

It has been said that the Highlands prior to the seventeenth century had a kinship society tinged by feudalism, as opposed to Lowland society where feudalism was tinged by kinship. Whether this is precisely true or not is open to argument but the reality of substantial social differences between the two areas can scarcely be questioned.

The topography of the Highlands and Islands lent itself to settlement by groups of families sharing small and often widely separated arable areas surrounded by extensive acreages of grazing. Although the precise system of sharing might vary, all such communities were co-operative organisations by any standard, in marked contrast to the individualistic crofting system which superseded them. The relationship between the clansmen tenants and sub-tenants, through the middleman to the chief was neither a simple economic one of landlord and tenant nor a mere military relationship of commander and soldier· it implied a complex set of mutual obligations and rights. Each community was highly self-sufficient and exports of cattle paid for limited imports which 'he region requ...ed.

The aftermath of the two principal Stuart rebellions intensified changes already taking place in Highland society as chiefs and their principal lieutenants began to indulge increasingly in activity outwith the region. The complex relationship between chief and clansman degenerated into a simple, and one-sided economic one, much to the bewilderment of the latter. The limited capacity of the area to generate cash income was increasingly devoted to the support of the chiefs' social aspirations in Edinburgh and London.

In some areas, a large labour force was a useful asset, permitting profitable labour-intensive activities such as the production of kelp. In other areas, cash income could be more readily achieved by adopting less intensive, and particularly less labour-intensive, forms of agriculture so that even if total output actually declined, local consumption by those needed to work the land declined still further and the balance of production available for sale increased.

The dramatic events in Sutherland and elsewhere which have been termed the Highland Clearances are well documented and widely known; what is not always equally appreciated is the extent to which the indigenous people throughout the region were driven from the land during the second half of the eighteenth century and the early part of the nineteenth by a long and undramatic process of attrition, including non-renewed leases and insupportable rent increases. For every man or woman recorded in the violent mass expulsions, there were many others equally dispossessed who have made little mark in the history books.

During the Napoleonic period as commodity prices rose, an insecure and irrational economy developed in the Highlands and Islands. Long-established economic patterns were replaced by new activities geared to exploit temporary opportunities and when peace came and many commodity prices fell, the region faced economic crisis. Simultaneously the industrial revolution was gaining in momentum in Scotland.

When the industrial revolution reached the Highlands and Islands, the region was already being opened up to Lowland influences and the transport revolution, in particular, provided the technology to accelerate the process. New roads and regular shipping services opened up new markets elsewhere in Scotland for the region's primary products and simultaneously gave access to the Highlands for the products of the new factory system at a time when specialised craft manufacture was barely established in the region.

In the early stages of the development of the factory system, new employment opportunities came to the Highlands, through linen manufacture for example, but this employment was shortlived and well before the middle of the nineteenth century the region had established an economic pattern which fundamentally remains to this day. Moreover, this pattern is largely the product of the revolution in agriculture, industry and transport which commenced two hundred years ago and in very few respects does it preserve features of the earlier Highland economy.

Economic Pattern Today

The first feature of this pattern is that the resources of the Highlands and Islands are largely concentrated in the hands of numerically insignificant minorities who continue to pursue a self-interest unequalled since the high-noon of *laissez-faire* economics.

Whilst the absentee landowner is readily identified as a culprit in the public view, other favoured minorities are not always recognised as sharing this privileged status nor is the detrimental effect of their activities on the community as a whole understood. There is little recognition, for example, that the grant-aided inshore fisherman who sells his catch to the klondyker is providing shore jobs in fish processing elsewhere at the expense of employment opportunities locally. It is even more remarkable to see the tolerance, indeed often public approval, of the activities of property owners, whether locally based or not, who subordinate the development of a balanced local economy to the success of their speculative schemes, even where such schemes yield quick and substantial profits to their sponsors without any new productive assets actually materialising or a single new job being created.

Traditionally, Highland communities survived in harder times and in a difficult and hostile terrain because they practised solidarity and co-operation. The few real economic success stories in the region in recent years have been greatly facilitated by community spirit and by individuals adopting far-sighted and unselfish strategies.

A second feature of the post-transformation situation in the Highlands, already briefly referred to, is the low level of regional self-sufficiency now achieved. Before the transport revolution opened up the area, a very high level of self-sufficiency was achieved and one might have expected this to be maintained, at least to some extent, in an area where money and employment were in short supply and where the economic advantages of large-scale manufacture elsewhere are offset, at least in part, by the very high costs of transport both to and within the region. That this did not occur can be attributed initially to the way in which the transport system developed in the Highlands. From the beginning, transport routes penetrated the region from outside centres and a pattern of feeder routes developed around each main inter-regional trunk route. Even today, there is no comprehensive *intra*-regional transport network in the Highlands and Islands: many journeys between two Highland communities are most readily accomplished via Glasgow or Aberdeen.

Consequently, although the region is populated by 250,000 people with many common or similar needs for goods and services, the absence of adequate transport within the region has inhibited the development of larger local markets for locally produced goods and services. In recent years, the common practice by manufacturers of branded goods of spreading transport costs evenly between all their customers has helped to keep down the Highland cost of living but only by removing one of the few inherent advantages of the local producer in the local market.

A third persisting feature of the Highlands and Islands has been selective emigration. The period of the transformation was marked by high birth rates and widespread dispossession of small tenants where the land was suitable for less labour-intensive cultivation. Some of the surplus was absorbed in the growth of small Highland towns and in new crofting communities often on very poor land, but many Highland people left the region, temporarily or permanently, in search of employment.

There is considerable evidence from parish registers and census data that the new occupations being created by the transformation were being filled by incomers who in their turn were replaced by further incomers. Only brief construction booms temporarily slowed the emigration of the indigenous community. In the aftermath of the transformation came a more stable pattern but one of chronic decline and continuing emigration.

The education system in the region came to acquire a justified reputation and many school-leavers went on to higher education — inevitably outwith the Highlands in the absence of facilities. Relatively few returned except to retire and the pattern continues to the present day of most unqualified school-leavers remaining in those areas of the region where employment is available and of most qualified school-leavers, throughout the region, leaving for higher education and for careers elsewhere. The high incidence of incomers in the limited professional employment available in the region continues despite the academic successes of the Highland's secondary education system. The impact of the loss of many of the most enterprising young people from the communities of the Highlands and Islands during the most active years of their lives cannot be overestimated and surely must be a significant factor in the lack of community self-confidence and enterprise which is prevalent in much of the region today.

Gaelic

Despite the lack of confidence in the region's ability to tackle its own situation and the chronic problems of emigration and under-employment, a separate and distinct culture, or perhaps more correctly a group of separate and distinct cultures, has survived in the Highlands and Islands and amongst those emigrants who have maintained their roots.

There is much sympathy in Scotland for the idea that this culture is a valuable, intrinsic part of the total identity of the Scottish people and if little can or should be done politically to promote the Gaelic ethos particularly, action can be taken and should be taken, to remove the obstacles threatening its survival. Whilst few would grudge the Gaelic language its preservation, opinion is sharply divided as to the place of Gaelic as a living language of everyday use. It remains the natural language of thought and of infancy only in the Western Isles and in isolated spots elsewhere and, of course, there are parts of the region where there is no Gaelic tradition at all.

Contrary to prejudices too often expressed, there is no evidence that bilingualism inhibits education: indeed the evidence is to the contrary. Very few would seriously suggest the promotion of Gaelic in the manner adopted by the Eire Government but Gaelic remains a living language, though a fragile one, and the opportunity still exists to maintain it as a living language in those parts of the Highlands and Islands where sufficient speakers reside. As a living language it can maintain its richness to an extent impossible as an academic or literary survival. And what is perhaps more important is that the prospects of establishing bilingualism are considerable in many localities where community self-confidence is at a low ebb.

Many would argue that current despair is not unrelated to the destruction of Gaelic as the predominant language in these localities by malevolent or ill-conceived policies, especially educational policies, in the past. If the attack on Gaelic has had a potent effect in undermining the traditional values of many Highland communities, perhaps it can equally be used as a symbol today to rebuild self-regard and self-confidence.

In an age when it was fashionable to look elsewhere for answers to Highland questions, a unique language was an obstacle to communication: in seeking salvation from local community resources it could prove to be an asset. In any case, it can do no harm to accept the enthusiasm of incomers to the Highlands who want to use Gaelic and the growing interest in Gaelic in Lowland Scotland at face value; it is for the Gael to use that support as he thinks best.

Community Dimension

If a future for the Gaelic and other distinctive cultures of the Highlands and Islands becomes an accepted national objective, the economic options available for revitalising the region are thereby significantly reduced. Whilst sympathetic incomers can participate in the regenerative process, their contribution must be integrated into that of the indigenous community.

Preferably the leadership and initiative should evolve from local sources; and by local sources one does not imply the public school educated, pseudo-Highland aristocracy. Where the source is external, local participation on local terms must quickly be recruited and developed. The nineteenth century transformation signally failed to involve the local community; indeed, successful indigenous projects such as the club farms in Morvern were deliberately discouraged or eliminated. In many cases, viable permanent immigrant communities were not successfully established and where permanence was achieved, the inplanted community generally failed to integrate with, or even to absorb, the indigenous community.

The importance of the community dimension of development has been missed by many of the well-intentioned, as opposed to the greedy, Improvers right down through early twentieth-century Improvers, such as Leverhulme, to the latter-day Improvers *par excellence,* the Highlands and Islands Development Board. However, a project which is unrelated to the development of the local community is more likely to attack the basis of that community's survival than to assist in the process of its development. It becomes merely a development geographically situated in the region: it·is *in,* not *of* the Highlands and Islands.

Once this basic principle is accepted, certain consequences follow fairly obviously such as questions of the balance of types of employment available locally or of competition for scarce local resources, to take just two examples. What is perhaps less obvious is that long-established norms of community social organisation may be in conflict with the normal patterns of leadership or interpersonal behaviour found in commercial and voluntary organisations elsewhere.

In recent years, several sociologists have commented on the horizontal as opposed to pyramidal structures of social organisation and cohesion within Highland communities. It is suggested that the dearth of truly indigenous entrepreneurs and the failure of many communities to take advantage of planning procedures to protect their interests are because both the "entrepreneur" and the "objector" roles are foreign to the established value systems of many Highlands and Islands communities.

Whilst it is easy to deny the existence of these hypothesised value systems or to write them off as being antiquated and needing change, it should not be forgotten that there are precedents which indicate clearly that economic development strategy and legal process can be modified to take proper account of community values. Collaborative development and innovation have worked well in the Faroes, for example, and the Land Court has shown a highly successful adaptation of judicial process. It would be ironic, to say the least, if at the very period when some of the most fundamental tenets of the western industrial tradition are being re-examined, and, in particular, the traditional power pyramid is being challenged by industrial democracy and by more participative styles of organisation, that the last vestiges of an older and proven set of participative social values were to be systematically destroyed to facilitate development ostensibly aimed at creating a viable economic basis for communities for which these social values still constitute a major *raison d'être*.

At first sight, the introduction of such complex and problematical sociological constraints may make one despair of the very possibility of the successful completion of a revitalisation process in the Highlands and Islands. But this is not necessarily the case for if the most viable communities can be stimulated into rejecting defensive (but historically justified) strategies and adopting positive and self-reliant attitudes towards self-management of innovation and of economic development, projects can be successfully initiated which will naturally and unselfconsciously incorporate the values of the sponsoring communities. This would, of course, depend on a sympathetic response from sources of capital such as the Highland and Islands Development Board.

Given even a few such successes initially and the continuing availability of relatively modest amounts of capital, the entire region could be revitalised within two decades by an internal transformation which could succeed where externally imposed development has failed, providing that the projects themselves are based on a realistic perception of the region and its prospects and providing that such enterprises receive priority access to the resources of the region.

Transport

The Highlands and Islands possess a number of distinctive features of which the cultural and social are only a part. An outstanding physical feature of the region is the matter of remoteness — not only of the remoteness from large centres of population elsewhere but the remoteness of Highland communities, and indeed of individual households, from one another. Remoteness is an inescapable function of the region's topography. Much of the land surface does not lend itself to settlement except on small and widely separated sites and much of the region's population lives on islands separated by stormy seas. Journeys between settlements are inevitably lengthened by difficult terrain and by the economics of providing transport facilities for relatively few people: these are the inevitable consequences of remoteness. In practise, however, journeys are frequently lengthened in distance and/or time by totally unnecessary difficulties. And the costs of transport are unnecessarily increased by bad transport planning.

It is quite beyond the scope of this paper to describe all the absurdities of Highland travel but mention should be made of the absence of a handful of transport links needed to complete a comprehensive network within the region, the lack of many suitably timed connections, the use of transport equipment inappropriate to the physical characteristics of the region or to the normal traffic volumes, the provision of competing, subsidised services where each could handle all the available traffic, and the unimaginative and uniform application of inappropriate transport regulations.

Many of these lunacies occur elsewhere of course, but there can be few areas where the results are more drastic or more apparent. The task of rationalising the situation is complicated by the multiplicity of agencies dealing with aspects of transport in the Highlands, almost all of whom appear to plan and operate while studiously ignoring the existence of the others.

39

Governments frequently justify their inability to change the situation on grounds of costs but, as in many other aspects of the Highlands and Islands, vast sums are already being expended on totally unsatisfactory services — sums which are more than enough to provide much superior services if they were spent sensibly.

Currently, around £100m is being spent improving the A9 between Perth and Inverness but approval was long withheld on a £3.5m scheme to produce at least equivalent improvements to the parallel stretch of railway line. A scheme is well advanced to provide a more direct road from Inverness to Easter Ross at a cost of perhaps £50m which will save perhaps 10 to 15 minutes car travel time over a relatively cheap upgrading of the existing road but provide few advantages to the very large proportion of travellers on the existing route who have intermediate starting points or destinations.

On the same route, three half-empty, inconveniently timed, slow trains per day compete with half-filled buses taking roughly twice the journey time on what could be the most heavily used public transport route within the region if served by frequent light rail cars supported by feeder bus routes. In all these cases, the better alternative would actually be cheaper to provide and to operate, which is by no means an unusual situation as Loganair has demonstrated to British Airways and Western Ferries to CalMac.

In a region such as the Highlands, the role of transport is absolutely crucial as it is by far the most significant, single, economic variable in so many situations.

Inevitably, transport will always pose greater problems in the Highlands and Islands than elsewhere in Scotland, but that is all the more reason for optimising the services that can be provided for the finance available and for adopting economic strategies which take advantage of the topography of the region.

Arguments about economies of scale can be overturned by high costs of transport, leading to the conclusion that production from local materials and/or for local consumption should have considerable advantages. Yet much industrial promotion in recent years has been directed to bringing industries to the Highlands and Islands which neither process local materials nor serve the local market and which consequently bear the double disadvantage of high transport costs in both directions. Meanwhile, the region continues to export predominantly primary products and to import goods and services capable of local production.

Population

Much interest has been focused on the population statistics of the region and pleasure has been expressed at the growth of population since 1961. Favourable conclusions are, however, based on more than dubious premises, for almost all the growth is attributable to the town of Inverness itself and when the growth of a few other sizeable communities is also taken into account, it is clear that the population of most of the Highlands and Islands continues to decline.

Moreover, the decline is occurring where loss of population is most damaging and where a modest growth would have the most beneficial effect. When one further considers that the estimated increase in the last few years is largely due to short-term, oil-related contracting, it is clear that the process going on today has ominous similarities to that which occurred in the early nineteenth century and from which the region has not yet recovered.

The Highland "Problem" is inseparable from the future of the outlying communities of the region. If Scotland needs another East Kilbride, it should be built at Stonehouse or elsewhere in the Lowlands; there is no economic rationale for building one in Easter Ross. But there is a rationale, if largely a cultural and social rationale, for giving self-sustaining vitality back to the Highlands and Islands again — a vitality taken from the region by converting it into a number of separate, if partly overlapping, sub-areas playing a satellite role to the advantage of the Lowland economy in general and to a privileged economic minority in particular.

Because the resources of the Highlands are scattered, its economic opportunities are scattered and its population must consequently be scattered too. With better use of these resources, outlying communities can grow and so acquire greater social as well as economic vitality. But it is not enough simply to exploit these resources. The benefits must be carefully channelled into the communities, and this will not occur as long as the enterprising local individual is denied access to these resources whether by large-scale landowners, inactive or absent crofter neighbours, unsympathetic government agencies or financially privileged outsiders seeking second homes or business opportunities.

The H.I.D.B.

The Highlands and Islands Development Board has been all too ready to welcome increased economic activity irrespective of the extent to which the indigenous community has participated. Numerous examples can be quoted such as the new, grant-aided hotel employing little or no local labour, purchasing all its equipment and supplies from outside Scotland (let alone the Highlands) and exporting its profits which are badly needed for reinvestment in the region. As such enterprises may well capture trade from established local businesses, their effect may be to siphon more cash out of the local economy than they introduce.

The Board may now be more aware of the lack of correspondence between local economic activity and local economic benefit and a recent Board publication tells the far from apocryphal tale of the island with a daily boat arriving in the morning with a cargo of tourists, in season, who departed in the early afternoon after making modest purchases in the island store. If the boat had been based on the island and its timetable reversed, island residents could have been employed on it and others could have shopped on the mainland without the cost of overnight accommodation. Moreover, a smaller number of tourists would have visited the island but probably have spent more, on bed and breakfast for example, and a smaller boat could have coped with the peak summer traffic so reducing year-round operating costs and possibly fares. It is exactly such optimising tactics that are so essential if outlying communities are to prosper.

Multi-occupation

Even if population growth occurs, many small communities will need services to an extent that does not justify the employment of even one full-time person to provide any one such service. Economists are inclined to turn up their noses at the idea of one person doing more than one job: this is apparently old-fashioned and therefore quite beyond the pale. Old-fashioned it may be but it makes good sense to many Highland communities where often the only feasible alternative is to forego the service altogether.

Multiple occupation still occurs widely in outlying communities but its continuance is threatened and its development circumscribed by rules and regulations which could be relaxed within the Highlands and Islands at little or no cost but with considerable benefit in terms of both increased services and employment. Multiple occupation can put together a satisfactory income from a number of different activities, perhaps seasonal in nature, which individually cannot provide an adequate living.

When one sees the hill farmer in the eastern Alps, his cattle safely in the byre for the winter, spending his day harvesting timber with his neighbour from the forest between his in-bye and his summer pasture, which protects their homes from avalanche and which removes much of the obtrusion of a thriving tourist industry largely in local hands, one begins to appreciate the scope offered by the integrated use of community-exploited resources and by multiple occupation. If these principles can be further combined with greater opportunity for self-employment, perhaps the problem of selective emigration can also be tackled and more enterprising young people will choose to make their futures in their own communities.

Education and Emigration

An ultimate solution to the problem of selective emigration will require substantial expansion of the very limited facilities for tertiary education available within the region and particularly education geared to the specific requirements of the Highlands and Islands. There is a need for professional education specific to the Highland situation: a teacher in a one-teacher school will almost certainly have been trained to cope with the problems of a large urban comprehensive; the training and experience of planners will normally be focused on new towns and urban overspill.

A primary aim of education in the region should be to equip school-leavers with the means to achieve a full life within the Highlands and Islands rather than to provide those vocational qualifications for which there can be no demand in the Highlands.

Efforts have been made in the past to establish a university in Inverness but there is now a growing and healthy scepticism about the value of such an institution and about the dangers of it becoming a university *in* the Highlands but not *of* the Highlands. There is no reason why an institution of higher education need be concentrated on a single centre; indeed the success of the Open University has clearly shown the potential of dispersed higher education. The adoption of a dispersal strategy would spread the very considerable benefits of such an institution more widely and might assist the parallel development of secondary education so that fewer Highland children, and particularly Island children, have to study away from home, a process which many believe sows the seeds of later emigration.

Agency Proliferation

There is a great proliferation of statutory agencies operating within the

Highlands and Islands. Many hoped that the Highlands and Islands Development Board would be given a co-ordinating role but in fact its task is largely to fill the gaps left by the other agencies. The co-ordinating role remains to be filled and the urgency grows greater. Ideally such a role should be filled by a body under democratic control but the Highland Regional Council gives little grounds for hope that, in the absence of grass-roots revival, a democratic forum for the entire Highlands and Islands would serve the interests of its communities rather than those of the vested interests which continue to dominate Highland affairs.

The transport problems of the region exacerbate the difficulties of voluntary organisations, such as local political groups, co-operating effectively throughout such a large area and the attempts of Labour, Liberal and S.N.P. to play a significant part in the first Highland Regional elections largely failed for this reason. Inevitably, the election was an overwhelming victory for the Regional Establishment, who also dominate official regional "pressure groups" such as consultative councils with predictable effect.

Only in the three Island authorities is the scale managable and the prospect hopeful. In the Highland Region in particular and in the Highlands and Islands area overall it may well prove better to build the future from the local, or district, level rather than at a Regional level but, in any case, the task remains almost certainly impossible in the absence of sympathetic action from national government.

Land Reform

An early priority must be land reform, not only because agriculture is a major element in the area's economy but because the fact of large-scale, monopoly landownership dominates many other aspects of the Highland scene. Large landowners exercise more complete planning and development control than local government planning authorities, have almost total control over local employment and housing availability, and have an influence over the democratic process unacceptable in the twentieth century. Much public anger has been expressed at the absentee landowner and at the deliberate underuse of land capable of agricultural or other development. In an island dependent on food imports and, more importantly, in a region of very limited economic opportunity, the rights of the landowner cannot include the right to deliberately waste the nation's resources.

A Land Use Commission is needed to encourage, and if necessary to coerce, the proper use of Highland land. But this is not enough in itself, for the local land monopolies must also be broken up to achieve viable local economies and vital democratic communities. It is no answer to replace the private monopoly of land by a public monopoly. Indeed, the large-scale public landowners in the Highlands have frequently collaborated with the private land monopolies and have shown a lack of sympathy for the local community interest.

There is a great need for integrated land use in the Highlands and for agriculture, forestry and tourism in particular to work in co-operation, not in competition. If a Land Use Commission becomes more than a transient owner of land, who can doubt that it will put organisational convenience before optimum land use as the Forestry Commission and other public agencies have done in the past? To combine regulatory powers over land with continuing ownership responsibilities is a recipe for failure.

Crofting

Current crofting reforms show a possible solution which would be widely welcomed: let the Land Use Commission acquire the large estates and make the agricultural land available as family-sized units for rent on a secure tenancy or for sale to practical farmers, let it provide generous loans and grants for improvements and let the Commission exercise a loose but effective control over changes of ownership to block the reaggregation of holdings and the re-creation of "private collective farms".

Critics of the current crofting reforms have expressed concern that newly created owner-occupiers will sell their land for development and take a quick but substantial profit so fragmenting crofting townships, or sell buildings as second homes at the expense of the local housing stock. The combination of community ownership of development land and the rigorous application of the Town and Country Planning Acts can obviate this danger, particularly if second or seasonal homes were to be made a separate use category from year-round inhabited housing for planning purposes.

Further refinements of planning legislation would also be helpful in achieving better land use as the existing system is focused on the release of land from agriculture to industrial, commercial and residential use and has little or no impact on changes of use between agriculture, forestry and recreation.

Even the creation of significant numbers of farm units capable of providing a substantial part of a family's income could have a revolutionary effect on large areas of the Highlands in combination with other part-time employment opportunities on local services, in tourism or in small-scale industry, or in forestry, for example. The creation of such employment would require fundamental reorientation of the policies of public bodies, such as the Highlands and Islands Development Board, putting more emphasis on the small-scale local tourist operator and the factory processing local produce, or the Hydro Board using the Highland's own resources to provide cheap power for the Highlands or the Forestry Commission re-examining its production-line, clear-fell methods. Such fundamental policy changes will only occur in response to specific government directives.

Fishing

Another early priority for government action, particularly in relation to the Islands, is establishing priority access for local fishermen, in the context of an overall policy of conservation of fish stocks. The plight of the Scottish inshore fishing industry in the face of widespread over-fishing by foreign vessels outwith current fishing limits is well known and the position may be no better if English distant water vessels turn to Scottish waters when 200-mile limits are established, despite their economic vulnerability due to their high capital costs. In any case, E.E.C. vessels, renowned for their short-sighted and rapacious fishing methods, will have access to Scottish inshore waters virtually without restriction after 1982.

It is not always realised that already much damage is done to inshore fisheries, including shell fisheries, even within current limits, around the Islands, by non-local boats or that historically, the rich fisheries off the west coast of Scotland made first Dutch, then Glasgow, entrepreneurs rich whilst conferring very few benefits on the communities of the Highlands and Islands.

Only urgent government action can give effective protection and priority to the fishermen of the region in their own immediate inshore waters. Only a co-ordinated scheme of conditional grants for vessels and of investment in on-shore facilities can generate the valuable spin-off of on-shore employment which today largely passes the region by.

Oil

Oil has been a major factor in the recent economic affairs of the region but even in Shetland, where the community has taken a series of confident initiatives to control the situation, widespread concern remains for the ultimate social and economic impacts. In other areas, it is already clear that the middle-term impact will be largely negative.

Temporary employment in contracting has masqueraded as permanent industrial development while less-well-paid, but secure, long-term employment has disappeared in circumstances in which its re-establishment is unlikely. Housing has been provided for permanent immigrants for whom there is no permanent employment and who will intensify local competition for employment when oil contracting goes. Public funds have been redirected from badly needed local infrastructure to meet the specific demands of the oil industry.

Oil contracting in the Highlands must only be permitted to continue in the context of full public information on its impermanence and plans must be made now to make good the damage that will occur as employment in this sector declines. An adequate proportion of the vast corporate profits and tax revenues arising from the exploitation of Scotland's North Sea Oil must be earmarked specifically for the needs of those areas which are most at risk.

Community-centred Development

The critical role of transport has already been stressed and the lack of co-ordinated capital expenditure and integrated services mentioned. Whatever steps are taken elsewhere in Scotland to co-ordinate transport, there is an urgent need for a government agency, answerable to democratic pressures, to perform a co-ordinating and integrating role for the Highlands and Islands.

Lack of capital has been a major cause, perhaps only second to the local land monopolies, of the lack of community-centred economic development in the past. The undiscriminating approach of the Highlands and Islands Development Board must be changed. The community aspect of development must be brought to the fore in giving priority to the indigenous project, in refusing the exploitative project from elsewhere and in playing a more direct role in initiating enterprises which would increasingly be transferred to local control as their success was established.

Development incentives must also be more discriminating in the balance of types of employment offered, particularly in the most populous parts such as Caithness, Easter Ross and Lochaber, if stable communities are to thrive where qualified school-leavers have the opportunity of suitable careers in their own locality.

Easter Ross, especially, prior to recent adverse publicity from oil-related activity, was very attractive to the professional in-migrant. After oil, much of this attraction could be re-established and if such expansion of professional employment is sensibly and responsibly handled, a situation can be developed where today's professional in-migrant is tomorrow's career opportunity for the local community.

Whilst Ross and Cromarty County Council fell over themselves to attract the possibility of thousands of temporary semi-skilled jobs, no effort appears to have been made to attract the drilling technology research centre, for example, and in the longer term the latter would have brought great benefits.

Whilst suitable policies in the fields of land use and ownership, access to, and control over, the other natural resources of the region and transport and development incentives are essential and a community-centred approach is indispensible, most vital of all is the need for a new self-confidence in the region, especially among younger people. If this community self-assurance fails to materialise, subsidies will continue to be directed towards the Highlands and Islands in increasing quantities only to end up, all too often, in the pockets of those who least need them.

SCOTLAND'S ECONOMY

Gavin Kennedy

Scotland Too Poor

The debate about the Scottish economy has followed the electoral wave of the S.N.P. In the mid-1960s the S.N.P. snatched the seat at Hamilton and the prospect of independence took on political credibility for the first time since the S.N.P. was founded in 1934.

Central to the debate was the issue of living standards before and after independence. Unionists asserted that Scotland, being the poorer relation of England, made it inevitable that she would suffer some loss of personal wealth on separation; the more extreme Unionists simply asserted that there was an annual direct transfer of resources from England to Scotland (a budgetary subsidy of a few hundred million pounds sterling) and that this proved a reduction in living standards would be necessary.

The S.N.P. replied to the debate by attempting to prove the contrary. Scotland was poor because of, not in spite of, the Union with England and that there was evidence on the sparse figures available that Scotland was actually making a budgetary contribution to the Union above its return from government expenditure — it was, in effect, subsidising England.[1]

The main problem in the debate was the dearth of statistics relating to the Scottish economy. The British government did not make the information it had available to the public, more I suspect out of disinterest than malevolence. Since 1972 it has altered this policy though the key statistics on Scottish trade are still not available nor has there been much official effort to collect them.[2] (The Input-Output Economic Model from the Fraser of Allender Institute at Strathclyde University should provide this information).

Like all political debates much nonsense was purveyed on all sides. Some Scots (few English politicians took the slightest interest in the matter) even rejected the whole idea of an independent Scotland on the dubious grounds that it was impossible! But the debate did not remain at this absymal level. In 1969, Dr Gavin McCrone (Oxford and Glasgow) published his contribution to the debate. This made no attempt to defend the economics of Unionism — total centralised decision-making — but argued instead for economic devolution. McCrone's main criticism was directed at "The Consequences of Separation".[3]

It is said of some senior civil servants that when they decide to stop a Minister doing something that he feels committed to they do not oppose him head-on. Instead, they break the Minister's resolve by raising practical problems (real and inspired) that lead to a qualification of the Minister's intentions; in effect, they frighten him with difficulties. This could be called death by a thousand exceptions. In illustration of this technique a small quotation from McCrone's book will suffice:

"Many people start discussing the economics of nationalism by asking if Scotland could be self-supporting. This is an absurd question. . . . Scotland has a highly industrialised economy with a gross domestic product per head which, though slightly less than England's nevertheless makes her comparable with other European countries. She is therefore among the more advanced nations of the world economically. She is clearly much wealthier than the Republic of Ireland and a thousand times more able to look after herself than Basutoland, which nonetheless manages to be independent. If Scotland becomes independent, no doubt a variety of adjustments would have to be made to her economy, some of which might be drastic and painful; but if Scotland wanted to be independent, there is obviously no question of her being unable to afford it economically."[4]

Thus, argues McCrone, Scotland could be economically independent if it wanted to, but "adjustments" would be needed and some of them would be "drastic and painful".

The rest of his book is directed at identifying the "adjustments". The practical reader is left in no doubt that the pain is unnecessary if only a simple adjustment, such as devolution, is made; this way, Scotland can get the benefits of the Union with England and the benefits of "Home Rule". The "adjustments", however, turn out to be arguable, rather than certain, particularly looking back on them from the vantage point of the last seven years.

McCrone was of the opinion that there was a budgetary transfer from England to Scotland of under £100m.[5] If we accept this figure it follows that an independent Scotland would either have to raise taxation and borrowing or cut public expenditure. Neither alternative being palatable it was a strong weakening blow at the resolve of Scots to be independent.

Scots, of course, could decide to risk the budgetary problems of unscrambling the Union and press ahead for independence on the grounds that political sovereignty would permit an independent economic policy and a chance to reorganise the economy in such a way that the economic gains from growth and full employment would meet the relatively small deficit of £100 to £200 million.[6] McCrone pointed out that the Scottish economy was too open to permit a really independent economic policy. The domination of Scottish trade and economic decision making by England was unlikely to be removed by independence, and what was worse, Scottish independence would remove a Scottish voice from the "Commanding Heights" of Westminster.

Practical difficulties were raised such as in the field of taxation and fiscal policies generally. The open border would lead to speculative transfers if Scottish and English taxes varied greatly. Closing the border to prevent this would mean retaliatory tariff and non-tariff action by London. This would hurt Scotland more than England it was alleged, though why McCrone and others are so sure that an English government would react in the sometimes petty ways that they suggest says much for their perception of the depth of inter-British friendship and goodwill.

Looking at the needs of Scottish manufacturing, McCrone found other practical difficulties. Scotland's economic position suggested that a devaluation would be beneficial. The older Scottish manufacturing industries were in the main uncompetitive with those in England and this explained the decline of

Scottish manufacturing over the years. An independent Scotland would be inclined on these grounds to try to devalue its currency in relation to England. The unemployed would provide the pool of labour from which the export growth could be built and Scotland could move towards full employment and a higher growth rate. The problem was that the English would not necessarily accommodate themselves to a Scottish devaluation and being stronger economically they could frustrate it. Sanctions could follow, such as a refusal of English capital for the necessary Scottish investment to finance the export expansion of manufacturing capacity.

The alternative to a Scottish devaluation, in these circumstances, was an intensification of Regional Policy and a surrogate devaluation by means of employment premiums, development grants and such like. Naturally, all this was possible within the framework of the United Kingdom, though why the English would be prepared to make the sacrifice needed to shift these resources to Scotland, in competition with the peripheral regions of England, and would not be prepared to accommodate to a Scottish devaluation, which meant a transfer by trade of English resources, remains a minor mystery.

McCrone's arguments were aimed at the costs of independence and showing that they could outweight any benefits. Independence was possible economically but not worth the cost because it could not solve the fundamental problem of the Scottish economy. Scotland was too weak, too poor and too vulnerable for it to opt for independence and maintain, let alone increase, its relative living standards.[7]

Scotland Too Rich

After the 1967 victory at Hamilton the S.N.P. stood still electorally. This victory had been enough, however, to move the Conservative and Unionist Party, under Edward Heath, in 1968 to set up a commission, chaired by Sir Alec Douglas Home, to look at devolution. The Labour Government with typical Wilsonian flair went one better and set up a Royal Commission. In the event at the 1970 General Election the S.N.P. increased its national vote but did not increase its parliamentary representation. The debate went into hibernation.

In 1974 two General Elections brought the nationalists back into political business. In February the S.N.P. took seven seats. In October it took eleven. Independence was once again on the agenda. The Tories came out in favour of a Scottish Assembly, albeit selected from the huge regional councils that had been established in Local Government reform. The Labourites went one better (of course!) and came out for an elected Scottish Assembly by 1976. The political arithmetic of the advance of the S.N.P. was clearing the minds of the Unionists.[8]

Two factors that assisted this process were the political force of the S.N.P. and the existence of large quantities of oil off the Scottish coast. It was necessary to meet the nationalist sentiments of the Scots by conceding the case for devolution (while trying to minimise the powers of the devolved Assembly) and to hang onto Scotland to claim sovereignty over the oil. The Yom Kippur War of 1973 led to the vast increase in the value of the oil reserves and an increase in their strategic importance. The then Prime Minister, Harold Wilson, claimed the oil off Scotland was worth £200 billion at 1974 prices and

49

estimates of the taxation revenue from the oil varied up to £3 billion a year (the 1976 official government figure).[9]

The S.N.P. was quick to seize on the implications of the oil. It undertook a vast propaganda drive among the Scottish people to bring home to them just how much oil was off Scotland's shores. The early S.N.P. estimates of £800m a year were derided by Unionist politicians as grossly exaggerated! The S.N.P. recognised that these sums were so vast that most people would not appreciate their significance to their lives and the consequent campaign to claim it was Scottish Oil and relate the expenditures involved to the lives of ordinary Scots was aimed at raising the confidence of the Scots in themselves and their future after independence. The Unionist response was first to dismiss the arithmetic and then to attack the morality. This came oddly from the British who had only recently ruled a *British* Empire, who were always first to defend *British* interests and who wanted the oil to be *British,* not European, let alone African, Asian or American.[10]

The S.N.P. demand is for a Scottish Government to exercise political sovereignty over the oil. This would mean control of exploration and extraction. It would settle the conditions under which people worked on the rigs and the safety measures needed to protect them, other sea users and the environment. Scotland would negotiate with the oil companies on exploration fees and on their returns from investment. It would certainly get a better deal than the Labourites and Tories got and would impose higher taxation than either have so far proposed.[11] Some Labourites have been conned into thinking that their Government in Westminster has a plan to nationalise the oil and they often confuse national acquisition of the oil (perfectly feasible and in my view desirable) and the nationalisation of the oil companies carrying on exploration. Setting up a state oil company to acquire technological expertise of the kind needed for the North Sea is no short-term matter; that it can be done is beyond question but that the Labourites will do it and the S.N.P. will not is the crassest of political nonsense of the moment.

But this aside, the question must be put: where does the oil leave an independent Scotland? Are the arguments of McCrone still valid? Is Scotland too poor to be free? The debate, however, did not begin again from where it had left off in 1969. The silence on the economics of nationalism from 1972 to 1976 was deafening. Dr McCrone had an honourable reason for his silence: he was now a senior civil servant in the Scottish Office and barred from public controversy. Others were not so excused.

In January 1976 the silence was broken. Christopher Smallwood (Oxford and Edinburgh) came forward with the argument that independence "was not worth the candle"[12] because the oil wealth made Scotland too rich to be free. It was the old argument of costs and benefits once again.

This time the devaluation that Scotland needed was prevented not by Perfidious Albion but by the oil wealth. The revenues would strengthen an independent Scottish pound and drive it up against the English pound. This revaluation would be by as much as 100 per cent. Such a movement in the exchange rates would deal a death blow to the Scottish manufacturing sector which was already declining and uncompetitive with England. Thousands of workers in manufacturing would lose their jobs because Scottish goods could not be sold abroad, nor at home because of cheaper imports from England.

Smallwood's arguments have been appearing in Parliament and the Scottish press with the regularity that is normally associated with an orchestrated P.R. exercise. However, this is not a serious complaint, after all, the S.N.P. would so the same, though hopefully with more justification. Edmund Dell, former Paymaster General in Wilson's Government, has been making the most mileage out of the revaluing currency scare and, being British, he naturally concludes that Scotland would be much better off to hand over its oil wealth to the British Treasury. In another paper in this volume, David Simpson suggests an alternative which is closer to Scotland's real interests.[13]

It is not sufficient to apply a text-book proposition on the mutual costs and benefits of a surplus and deficit on the balance of payments. The experience of the falling pound sterling (under $2 to the pound and moving towards $1) has not been conducive of text-book confidence in the benefits of devaluation. The efforts of the British Treasury to push the economy towards a balance of payments surplus does not lend support for the proposition that a Scottish surplus would be catastrophic for the economy. Indeed, I know of no country in the world that would eschew the opportunities created by a balance of payments surplus and I can conceive of no economics ministry that would be so manifestly incompetent that it could not handle the problems created by the tendency of its currency to become undervalued. In fact, given a choice, Mr Dell and his colleagues would regard it as a proof of good fortune, or even good judgment, if they could manage an economy with the terrible burdens that they forecast for an independent Scotland in the matter of a surplus on the balance of payments and an undervalued currency. Their polemics against independence on this score have the hallmarks of warning the Scots about the evils of the pox while doing their damndest to catch it themselves.

Scotland Too Dominated

Regional economic policies have at least one virtue: they are evidence that something needs to be done. British governments have been trying regional policies for 40 years. The early attempts were little more than inadequate relief for the worst areas of the depression and were crippled by the nonsensical economic orthodoxy of the British Treasury and the credulity of the Ministers who took its advice.[14] After the war, Labour went for a policy of redistributing industry, since rationalised as an economic policy though at the time it was heavily influenced by the need to disperse industry following the experiences of target-bombing. This meant that in Scotland the Clyde Basin, Dundee and Inverness were scheduled to receive new factory buildings under the auspices of the British Board of Trade. Industrial Development Certificates were created to direct industry into the scheduled areas.

Each government tried its own policies. The Tories went for growth points in 1963. Labour went for Development Areas, investment grants and regional employment premiums. The Tories returned to investment allowances but switched back to grants. Finally, the clear need for substantial investment turned Labour to a Scottish Development Agency. On top of all these direct measures all governments found it increasingly difficult to allow major enterprises in the development areas to go bankrupt and the policy of supporting "lame ducks' was instituted.

Whatever the inadequacies of regional policy at any one time there is no doubt that it has had some effect. It is possible, for example, to argue that things would be much worse without a policy. But one thing is also inescapable: *regional policy has been an instrument for the industrial colonisation of Scotland.*

The Labour Party has made much of its commitment to regional policy. Its spokespersons tend to parade the record as if it is an unmitigated virtue. This, of course, they are entirely at liberty to do on the grounds that their policy for Union is supported by their faith in the efficacy of regional policies. In passing we ought to note the political effect of regional economic policies as applied to Scotland. Socialists and social democrats react to regional policy in one of two ways. There are those who believe that the Scottish problem can be solved if only the regional policy is pursued vigourously enough by Westminster. For them it is all a question of scale. Therefore they are in favour of Union on the grounds that their lobbying powers with Westminster are enhanced by their presence there.[15] In their view their role is to see that Scotland gets "its" share of whatever I.D.C. awards are made. In return they deliver the Scottish vote to the Labour Government. The other group take a different view of regional policy but end up with the same political conclusion. For them regional policy has been a failure. Scottish industry has failed to make progress even with the entire battery of regional assistance available to it. Millions have been poured into Scottish industry and millions more is available but indigenous industry is just incapable of standing up to the competitive world. If Scottish industry cannot make a go of it with all the assistance available it is beyond doubt that independence would be an economic disaster. With this assistance Scotland is barely slowing down the slide backwards; without it there would be a greased slope to economic collapse. The political conclusion is that Scotland must get as close to England as possible. Devolution is viewed with suspicion.[16] In return for this integrationist programme these Labourites also deliver the Scottish vote, and they join their colleagues in waiting for socialism, or the social democratic corporate state, to solve everything.

The Labour Party has gone one step further than parading its regional policy. It has used its major consequence as an argument against independence. Scottish manufacturing industry is dominated by English and foreign control. Only 41 per cent of manufacturing employment in Scotland is in indigenous corporations. Of the rest, 40 per cent is controlled by English companies with their head offices and decision centres in England, 15 per cent is controlled from North America, 1.5 per cent from the E.E.C. and the balance from the rest of the world or through joint ownership with Scottish companies.[17]

In examining the nature of this domination important features become apparent. If the enterprise is large it is more likely to be controlled externally; Scottish enterprises tend therefore to be smaller. Branch plants of English and foreign corporations account for a quarter of manufacturing employment; what these corporations decide can have substantial effects on Scottish employees. Nearly half of all manufacturing employment is under the control of just 110 companies; this is measure of the size of the commanding heights of the economy. The faster the sector is growing (which generally means the most technologically and commercially viable corporations) the less likely is it that

Scottish control is important. Indeed, in the five fastest-growing sectors indigenous control accounts for less than 14 per cent of employment.[18]

This situation is turned into an argument against independence on the grounds that "it is almost impossible for an independent Scottish government to run an independent economic policy" and that "the power of Scotland to shape or even strongly influence her own economic future has been, is being, and probably will continue to be, strongly eroded".[19]

Yet it is Labour's regional policy of moving investment to the developing areas that is creating the colonisation that is being complained about. Labour is handing over control of the Scottish economy to the very multi-nationals which its spokespersons are often making speeches against. Labour is placing the welfare and employment of the majority of the Scottish people into the hands of the multi-nationals and insisting at the same time that its regional policies are a cause for congratulation and support at the polls! The irony of what the socialists are doing to Scottish working people is apparently not perceived even by those who tell us that "marxist consciousness" is a prelude to action. Rather they insist that Scotland should be grateful for more of what it has been getting.

Illustrative of this myopia and false perception we can turn to two recent struggles against unemployment. The Upper Clyde Shipbuilders' fight for jobs was led by members of the British Communist Party and supported, quite rightly, by Labourites, socialists and nationalists all over Scotland. Labour Minister, Anthony Wedgewood Benn, appeared with the sit-in leaders at demonstrations and pledged full support for the fight. The result was that the yard was bailed out not by a workers co-operative, nor indeed a labour-managed enterprise, but by a multi-national company from Texas. This was a victory? A Scottish government would have handed over the yard to a Scottish company, specially formed with public resources and distinguished by being managed by the employees.

If we take another example, the Chrysler Corporation at Linwood and the Leyland plant at Bathgate. Linwood was saved not by the struggles of Labourite M.P., Norman Buchan, eloquent and sincere as he is, but by the political realities of the S.N.P. threat to Labour in Scotland. Much has been made, and will continue to be made, of the S.N.P. demand that Linwood must *not* be treated in the usual manner of branch factories in Scotland when there is trouble in the English or foreign-owned company, namely, to shut them down first. If it had been a question of closing the British operation altogether and transfering European work to France (Simca) or back to America, Mr Buchan and his colleagues would have demanded closures elsewhere to protect British jobs. They would do this because they are British and feel responsible to British employees. Indeed, something like this has happened in the transfer of production from France to England of a new model which must inevitably mean fewer jobs in France and more jobs in England. A Scottish government would have had the option of creating an indigenous motor vehicle industry out of Linwood and Bathgate and, with investment in engine-building capacity, would have preserved employment on a far more secure basis than relying, as the socialists have agreed to do, on the mercies of the multi-national Chrysler Corporation.[20]

Domination of Scottish industry is a reason for independence not an obstacle. The financial, capital, taxation and profit-repatriation arrangements agreed to by the British government with multi-national companies are no exhibition for their guardianship of Scottish interests and the legitimate interests of those employed by them.[21] The British government is handing over Scotland to external forces of economic control with a determination to succeed that suggests if you want to make Scotland safe for the multi-nationals vote for the British connection.

A Scottish Government would have to adopt a positive policy towards external control of the economy. There is no question of banning all foreign investment. From a technological view that would be short-sighted. Even the Stalinists in the Kremlin have realised the folly of total exclusion. But all multi-nationals (English or foreign) would have to conform to Scottish laws on how they operate (employee management), on their incorporation within Scotland with indigenous control, on their pricing policies and the elimination of transfer pricing, on proper assessment for taxation and remitted profits, and on their conforming to Scottish economic planning. The objective would be to force such foreign corporations as were accepted to locate integrated operations in Scotland, running from research and development through to production and marketing, and to fit in with Scottish needs as determined democratically in Parliament. Corporations that were unwilling and unable to agree to the conditions of operation would be unwelcome.

Domination of national economic activity has been a cause of many of the nationalist struggles in the developing countries against imperialist and external economic control. The British Left has a long record of support for the principle of political independence in the Third World. Their supporters in Scotland would do something to redress their shameful record on Scottish independence by fighting for these same rights in their own country.

Scotland's Prospects

It is not possible to draw up a detailed blueprint of the economic policy of a radical Scottish government. A great deal will depend upon when independence takes place and the conditions under which the world economy is operating. The S.N.P.'s commitment to a negotiated separation of political powers means precisely what it says: everything is negotiable except the end result. Making predictions about what kind of economic policies follow from these negotiations would be idle speculation. Economists are poor predictors and most other people are not much better.

However, we can sketch in the main features and point to objectives and methods. This will not satisfy everybody but then what does? The over-riding commitment must be to full employment and ending for ever the use of unemployment as a lever of aggregate demand management. The original idea of Keynesian economics was to use aggregate demand to maintain full employment; only in the impossible British economy and the impenetrable mysteries of the British Treasury was it possible to reverse the relationship. On independence Scotland's work people will no longer be available to take the heat out of England's affluence.

No modern economy can operate, or indeed benefit from, *laissez-faire* capitalism. That a market has its uses is not challenged and any sensibly planned economy would use markets to test for efficiency and as a substitute for bureaucratised administration. But the open-season, anything-goes, catch-as-catch-can, let prices-rule system of industrial and commercial capitalism has no place in the economic management of a small country. The re-structuring of the Scottish industrial base will take some element of planning. Re-building the urban infra-structure of west central Scotland and, of course, other urban centres across the country, will require planning. But there is no need to adopt a Stalinist-type master-plan on the scale of Eastern Europe. The government can set out the broad outlines of what it believes is necessary (tested by critical scrutiny from a powerful parliament, independent of the Executive) and create special (but not necessarily permanent) agencies to implement these outlines and direct events. In their papers in housing and health in this volume, Colin Bell and David Hamilton have made suggestions on these lines. Similar proposals have been made elsewhere for education, industrial investment, agriculture, fisheries and so on.

The principle of decentralisation and devolution would be a feature of this planning phase for the transition to an independent economy. One of the problems of both the so-called free market and the social democratic state is the tendency to form ever-larger units. Bureaucratic centralism is the inevitable result of corporate mergers and the acquisition of functions by government. The two most dominant trends of the last century have been the concentration of competitive industry (e.g., the 110 corporations dominating Scottish manufacturing) and the extension and deepening of the functions of the State. The radical solution is to reverse the process.

Private oligopolies have provoked anti-trust legislation in mixed economies and also have led, lamentably, to their replacement by monopolistic state corporations. Why the Left remains so attached to nationalisation as an alternative to monopoly capitalism can have little to do with experience. British nationalisation has provided no grounds for having more of it in Scotland. The effect to date on Scotland's railways, coal, gas, electricity, and steel do not augur well for the prospect of British Leyland, British Oil and British Shipbuilding.

The management of economic resources does not require vast co-ordinating bureaucracies that file and re-file memoranda. Managements can be given responsibility to use resources for given purposes against a set of criteria that can be determined to suit the nature of the operation. The "ownership" of productive assets by shareholders is an anachronism and effectively of little importance even in a mixed capitalist-state economy. In the case of the State, "ownership" is also functionally meaningless. Labour management of productive resources can and should be developed so that all who operate the resources share in the control and management of them and take full responsibility for their use on behalf of the community.[22] If their enterprise fails the resources can be re-assigned or handed over to another labour-management team. This is in effect what happens in all industrialised economies at present, except that each malfunctions in ways according to the mythology of ownership that predominates. In capitalist societies management teams "bid" for control by mobilising the largest shareholders and lose their control if they go bankrupt. In socialist societies the State Bureaucracy assigns managements and re-assigns them. In both societies the employees and the consumers are dominated by the controllers of the productive resources.

In a radically managed economy producer control is shared by all employees and is charged with serving the community by providing it with goods and services at prices that reflect costs (including rewards to enterprise) and in conditions that meet high standards of safety, environmental protection and good quality. People who waste society's resources and serve themselves at the expense of others are not rewarded. If society wants to provide goods and services at less than the real cost then it does so by democratic decision and full knowledge of the economic consequences. Thus, the living standards of all can be raised and maintained at a level that reflects the meaning of a socially just society. This implies, and indeed demands, the liquidation of the inordinate inequalities of wealth and income that is common to both capitalist and socialist societies at present.

Scotland will be able to make major inroads in wealth inequality by breaking the economic power of the landed estates, often in foreign ownership, and terminating the system of private *ownership* of public resources, which includes unearned income from previous wealth accretions and, sadly, most recently, the acquisition of wealth-creating power in the public sector. Investment capital can still be mobilised from the savings of people through non-state banks and through a public bank or banks. Investment in an enterprise will not confer *ownership* of the business by the investor, merely a right to a return on the investment (up to some limit). The other source of investment capital would be from the retained earnings of the enterprise, voted on and agreed to, by the employees. Income differentials would have to be agreed with the work force and this should check abuses by minorities, either on the shop floor or in the Managing Board.[23]

Scotland would not be turned into a little Switzerland, full of speculators, merchant banks and finance manipulators.[24] Neither would it become a massive inter-locking state bureaucracy — Strathclyde Regional Council writ large. The institutions of the radical economy would be manageably small, democratic and responsible. Industrial investment would raise productivity and the earnings of employees. Exports would be geared to pay for those imports deemed necessary and would not become an end in themselves which normally ends in them being permanently insufficient to cover the inevitable imports brought in by the removal of domestic production to other countries. Total self-sufficiency is neither possible nor perhaps desirable but the broad objective would be to reduce dependence on imports by making the imports justify themselves as being necessary rather than inevitable. There is no reason why Scotland cannot have a high standard of living, with considerable variety in consumption goods, at some level of imports well below that presently experienced by Britain.[25]

The economic debate has moved on a long way since the argument about independence lowering living standards of the Scottish people. The threat of tariff retaliation by England has been removed by the accession of Britain to the E.E.C. Unless and until Scotland decides to leave the E.E.C. independence will include Scottish membership. Suggestions that independence means Scotland Out and England In are absurd; there is nothing in the Treaty that states that Britain joining meant that England would inherit membership and Scotland would not. Membership has many disadvantages, not least in fisheries, energy and aspects of agriculture, (though the common Agricultural

Policy works against the heaviest food importer, England), but there are also advantages. Trade between England and Scotland would not be interrupted because of the E.E.C. and the spectre of customs posts is as vacuous as that of Brittania ruling the waves.

The experience of economic life in the E.E.C. is that several countries with open trade and a common tariff can operate with different economic policies, different exchange rates, different strengths in their currencies, different taxation systems, different regional incentives, different phases of demand management, different languages, different monetary units, different foreign policies, different defence policies, different laws, different ideas and different ambitions. If the E.E.C. can work in this context why should Scotland and England have so much difficulty surviving as good but independent neighbours, with their common heritages, their common language, their common outlook and above all their common sense?

1 See T. L. Johnston, N. K. Buxton, D. Mair, *Structure and Growth of the Scottish Economy*, London, 1971, pp 169-182.

2 Scottish Office, *Scottish Economic Bulletin*, Edinburgh, Series 1972-

3 Gavin McCrone, *Scotland's Future: the economics of nationalism*, Oxford 1969.

4 Ibid, p 52; McCrone is, of course, absolved from any suggestion that he has put this technique to use in his professional capacity; his book is an isolated lapse illustrating the bad habits of others.

5 Recent work at Dundee University has produced a figure as high as £600m not all of which can be accounted for by inflation. See Begg, Lythe *et at, Expenditure in Scotland 1961-1971*, Edinburgh 1975. The Dundee method is to use the Keynesian identity: $Y = C + I + G + (X - M)$, where Y = national income, C = consumption, I = private investment, G = government expenditure, X = exports, and M = imports. If Y, C, I, G, are known, the residual, positive or negative, must equal the trade surplus or deficit respectively. The deficit does not necessarily imply dependence because the economy may be being managed in such a way that adjustments cannot take place through an exchange rate change or the economy could be starved of investment capital that makes the imbalance inevitable. Independence could alter the value of I and G through a heavier commitment to capital formation than Union, a Regional Policy and the S.D.A. are able to muster.

6 Recent statements by Labourites that the oil revenues in an independent Scotland would go down the "deficit drain" make remarkable reading when it is realised how small this deficit really is and how large the revenues will be. It is also relevant to note that Britain intends the oil revenues to plug the trade deficit of the U.K., currently running at over £1 billion, and pay off the heavy international borrowing entered into by the Government.

7 In a more recent paper on the problems of Scotland McCrone argued strongly for substantial investment in Scotland to offset the productivity gap with the U.K. The Scottish Development Agency is presumably a product of this thinking, though its ambitions exceed its current resources. See Gavin McCrone, "The Determinants of Regional Growth Rates", 1972, Mimeo for conference of the Royal Economic Society, Durham.

8 See Gavin Kennedy, "Scotland and Europe", *New Europe*, Janaury 1976.

9 For a discussion of alternative estimates see: Tom McRae, *North Sea Oil and the Scottish Economy*, Fletcher Paper no. 2, Edinburgh 1976; also in *Question*, March 1976; Speech by Harold Wilson at opening of B.P. pipeline, Aberdeen 1975.

10 Consider, for example, Prime Minister James Callaghan's performance on the subject of British Oil prior to the Energy Conference in Paris in 1975.

11 For an account of the S.N.P.'s position on the oil see: S.N.P. Research Department, *Scotland's Oil: The Background*, Edinburgh 1975; see also: Aberdeen Peoples Press, *Oil Over Troubled Waters: a report and critique of oil developments in North East Scotland*, Aberdeen 1976, for a detailed and critical account of the impact of the oil; this should be compared with earlier accounts: Royal Scottish Geographical Society, *Scotland and Oil*, Teachers' Bulletin, no. 5, Edinburgh 1973, and D. I. MacKay and G. A. Mackay, *The Political Economy of North Sea Oil*, London 1975.

12 Christopher Smallwood, "Economics Case for Independence", The *Scotsman*, January 1976, also: "The Economics of Separatism", Mimeo. Mr Smallwood worked for 18 months in the Devolution Unit set up in the Cabinet Office during 1974-75; his views naturally do not necessarily reflect those of his former colleagues.

13 An S.N.P. internal committee, chaired by Douglas Crawford M.P., produced two documents "Financial Management After Self-Government" and "Economic Development after Self-Government" (1975) which also put forward proposals to deal with the currency situation. The furore in the far left press over these proposals was somewhat tongue-in-cheek as all these groups encourage Scottish voters to support a Labour Government that pursues a far more conservative monetary policy than advocated by the so called right-wing S.N.P., but then consistency is neither necessary nor sufficient to participate in British politics.

14 For a readable account of the inter-war debate see Michael Stewart, *Keynes and After*, London, second edition, 1972.

15 John P. Mackintosh M.P. is probably best identified with this view as a maximalist devolutionist in the Labour Party. This commitment did not stop him defending the original minimalist White Paper proposals on devolution, which even the Scottish Council of the Labour Party decided were insufficient.

16 This was represented up to December 1975 by Robin Cook M.P., and perhaps best at the moment by Norman Buchan M.P. For S.N.P. views on devolution see: S.N.P. Research Department, *The Devolution White Paper: synopsis and commentary*, Edinburgh 30/1/76.

17 See Labour Party, *Labour's Analysis of the Economics of Separatism*, Glasgow 1976, (produced by a Committee chaired by Professor Adam Thompson of Glasgow University); see also: John Firn, "External Control and Regional Policy", in Gordon Brown, editor, *The Red Paper on Scotland*, Edinburgh 1975, pp 153-169.

18 Firn, Ibid, p 162.

19 Firn, Ibid, p 169.

20 It is also worth noting that the British Left's demand on the Labour Government to impose import controls is in effect a demand that foreign workers should be unemployed at the expense of British workers. Squaring this defence of British workers against foreign workers (many of whom are in the poor Third World) with an attack on the S.N.P. for defending Scottish workers requires a Stalinist mentality of truly Orwellian dimensions.

21 Even in negotiations with the oil companies the mighty British Government has come off worse than the Shetlander's local authority. Could a Scottish government do worse?

22 See Jaroslav Vanek, *Self-Management: economic liberation of man*, London 1975; this book gives socialist interpretations of labour-managed enterprises though no socialist society so far has institutionalised a fully democratic decentralised system of labour-managed production, mainly because it conflicts with the basic drive of state socialism, namely, to enhance the powers of state bureaucracy against the interests of the people.

23 The need to re-invest out of enterprise income to keep the business going and the certainty of frictional unemployment if the business folds through diverting enterprise income inordinately into personal earnings will prevent excessive and unjustified income demands by the employees. If no single company dominates the market for a product it will not be possible to pass wage hikes on as price increases and strong anti-collusion laws will prevent inter-company oligopolies. State monopolies will require special legislation; large manufacturers will be subject to the discipline of international competition.

24 The British Left in Scotland are over-fond of attacking the S.N.P. on these grounds, usually with reference to Sir Hugh Fraser of the House of Fraser who is not in the leadership of the S.N.P., nor active in its committees and has no influence on its policy-making. The Left should be more concerned about leading activitists of the British Labour Party who are financiers, large-scale property owners, land reclaimers, and industrial and commercial capitalists. The S.N.P., being a *national* party seeking constitutional change, is open to all who want to join it for this objective; so far the industrial and commercial classes have opted for Unionism which is already turning Edinburgh into a banking and financial centre out of foreign capital and Scotland's assets. Voting Labour in Scotland will never change that trend; it is in fact a precondition for it continuing.

25 Britain opted for cheap food imports and dependence on imports of raw materials paid for by exports of manufactured goods and earnings from being the world's banker and insurer. This worked in the 19th century when Britain was the workshop of the world and a leading innovator. Since the war, Britain has been unable to make its system balance. In 1955, 75 per cent of British imports were food and raw materials. Manufactured imports accounted for 5 per cent of the total and imports of semi-manufactures 20 per cent. By 1971, food and raw materials were only 50 per cent of total imports and imports of finished manufactures had risen to 24 per cent. Thus, half of all British imports by 1971 were in finished and semi-finished manufactures, the very commodities that Britain was dependent upon to pay for its food and raw materials. Over 85 per cent of all British exports are manufactured goods. Worse still, the world position of sterling

has diminished Britain's capacity to fund the deficit (though it still does remarkably well considering). As Britain exports more and more of its domestic product to pay its way, borrowing when it is in deficit, the earnings from exports are spent on importing the very commodities she is exporting. Scotland does not need to import the same proportion of its food needs as England and can export a healthy food surplus at present to gain variety (what it would achieve if it set agriculture to work would make this even better), nor does Scotland have England's appetite for imported energy. This must make Scotland's prospects more credible than England's.

Andrew Fletcher Society

The Andrew Fletcher Society was formed in 1974 to provide a forum for discussion and debate on the problems and opportunities of an independent Scotland. It does not take a collective view on any issues raised. It meets regularly in Glasgow and Edinburgh to discuss papers prepared on a variety of topics. Recent papers read to the Society include: Community Health, Defence, the Arts, Energy, Industrial Development, Housing, Social Democracy and Voting Patterns.

The Society publishes papers read at its meetings in the Fletcher Paper series. Those already published are:

No. 1 **The Defence Budget of an Independent Scotland**
Dr Gavin Kennedy
No. 2 **North Sea Oil and the Scottish Economy**
Professor Tom McRae
No. 3 **Scotland and Energy**
Dr Malcolm Slesser
No. 4 **Independence and Federalism after the Referendum**
Professor Neil MacCormick

Membership details can be obtained from **The Secretary, 33 Midmar Gardens, Edinburgh, EH10 6DY.**

Fletcher Papers (50p including postage) are available from **The Treasurer, 4 Doune Terrace, Edinburgh, EH3 6DY,** Cheques/P.O.s payable to Andrew Fletcher Society.

E

SCOTLAND, ENGLAND AND NORTH SEA OIL

David Simpson

The discovery of oil in the Scottish waters of the North Sea, which in political terms dates from around 1972, has had a remarkable effect on Scottish-English political relations. While it has strengthened the growing interest within Scotland in political independence, it has simultaneously created in England a resistance to the idea of Scottish Independence, a resistance which previous to 1972 could hardly be said to exist.

The Conflict of Interest

The principal factor in the movement towards self-government appears to have been the replacement of a British by a Scottish identity, a process similar to that which can be detected in such countries as Australia, New Zealand and Canada. But in Scotland the movement was contained by the fear that independence would mean a serious fall in the standard of living. That this fear was wholly without foundation did not make it any the less real. The discovery of oil has virtually abolished this fear, and with it the principal political constraint on the movement towards independence. But it would be wrong to suppose that independence is equated with instant oil wealth: on the contrary, many nationalists would gladly trade oil for independence.

On the other hand, Scottish independence is seen in England principally in terms of the fear that the loss of North Sea oil reserves would put in doubt the capacity of the British Government to repay, or re-finance, the heavy external borrowings of recent years. The oil reserves in what is now the British sector of the North Sea would almost certainly in the eyes of international law become the property of a Scottish government upon the creation of a sovereign Scottish state. Thus, the discovery of oil appears to have set the stage for a major conflict of interest between the two countries where none before was seen to exist. It seems to be commonly supposed that the conflict of interest can be cast in the form of a zero-game; whatever Scotland gains England must lose. All that can then be negotiated is the percentage share of a fixed sum.

This paper is designed to argue that the conflict may not be as direct as is commonly supposed, to the extent that England's interests lie primarily in the direction of access to a large pool of foreign currency with which its international debts can be settled, whilst Scotland's interests lie in the acquisition of real resources which can be used to reconstruct its economy and to provide a measure of political influence in international bargaining. The scheme which is proposed in the following pages is cast in terms of England having access to the foreign exchange, while Scotland has access to the real resource content of the oil revenues. In practice, of course, England will want some of the real resources and Scotland will want some of the foreign exchange, but the presentation here is deliberately simplified in order to get across the main point, which is that there can exist some arrangements according to which the interests of the two countries may be complementary rather than conflicting. Nor is it intended that the scheme which is described below should be taken too literally: it is merely a sketch of the possibilities and is open to a wide range of modification in practice.

The Proposal

It should be made plain that the difference in size, (England's population being roughly ten times that of Scotland), accounts for a great difference in the potential impact of the oil revenue upon the two countries. In Scotland's case, the officially estimated tax revenues from the oil will amount in the early 1980's to about 50 per cent of her G.D.P., while the same sum amounts to less than one third of the U.K. public sector borrowing requirements. Thus, while the oil revenues completely alter the prospects for rebuilding the Scottish economy, they can only be of limited relevance in solving England's economic problems.

Let us suppose that the share of the foreign exchange earnings which accrue from the export of oil to a sovereign government, (Scottish or British), will be £3 billion per annum, (£1 billion = £1 thousand million). This is still the official British estimate of the government's expected total tax receipts from the British sector of the North Sea from about 1980 onwards, after all expenses (including interest payments and capital repayments) have been met. Other estimates have ranged as low as half of this figure, but the principle of the following argument is unaffected by the size of the revenues.

Suppose further that a sovereign Scottish state comes into existence in 1980 and that the oil revenues accruing to the state are paid in dollars (or some other acceptably hard international currency) into an account jointly held by the Bank of England and the Central Bank of Scotland. Then the following arrangements might be agreed: that the Bank of England may draw on this account whenever it requires foreign exchange with which to repay its international obligations, up to an agreed maximum limit. Whenever it makes a drawing on this account, however, it must transfer an equivalent amount in pounds sterling, (at a rate of exchange to be agreed in advance), to another account held by the Central Bank of Scotland. The Central Bank of Scotland would then be free to dispose of its sterling account together with its own portion of the joint foreign currency account according to the principles of economic policy laid down by the Scottish government.[1]

In the following paragraphs we outline the consequences — both for the Scottish and the English economies — of the different ways in which these accounts might be used. Before passing on, it should be noted that we are assuming a flexible rate of exchange between the Scottish pound and the pound sterling, and between the pound sterling and other major currencies. Provided that the pound sterling is not expected to fall significantly in value relative to other currencies, it should be possible to agree in advance the special fixed rate at which "oil dollars" are to be converted into pounds sterling for the use of the Scottish Central Bank.

Use of the Revenues

There are broadly three ways in which sterling funds deriving from the oil revenues could be used:

(a) They could be devoted to purchasing material goods and services from current production in England.

(b) They could be devoted to the purchase of existing assets, (land, property, factories, etc.) owned by sterling holders both in Scotland and abroad.

(c) They could be devoted to a loan from the Scottish to the English government.

The foreign exchange held in the joint account and not taken up by the Bank of England could be transferred to pounds sterling, invested, lent abroad, given away as foreign aid, or used for acquiring goods from overseas.

The amount of the sterling funds which could be devoted to (a) would be limited by the capacity of the Scottish economy to absorb goods and services, and the capacity of the English economy to deliver them without undue strain. From the viewpoint of the Scottish economy the most likely short-run constraint would be the available labour supply: rather a change from the old Scottish employment problem! Full employment of labour would limit the capacity to absorb capital goods: there would be no such constraint (except prudence) on the capacity to absorb consumer goods. Indeed, one of the interesting questions which we shall not elaborate upon here, because it deserves a large study in itself, is the type of goods which should be imported.

I hope that it will prove possible to persuade voters to accept a high proportion of capital goods, rather than consumer goods, so that a foundation can be secured for the prosperity of future generations when the oil revenues have run dry. From the point of view of the English economy, it might be reasonable to expect it to be capable of exporting something of the order of £1 billion worth of additional goods and services to Scotland per annum. This would represent around 10 per cent of its 1973 level of exports of goods and services. A 10 per cent increase in exports would of course stimulate the level of aggregate demand in England, but it would nonetheless represent a real burden on the economy of that value, unless resources hitherto unemployed were brought into production.

The acquisition of (b), existing assets, could begin in Scotland with the purchase of ownership of the large tracts of land which are in non-Scottish hands as well as the acquisition of minority or majority shareholdings in productive enterprises operating in Scotland. Some of these transactions would have to be carefully considered from the political as well as from the economic viewpoint before being carried out. One of the obvious implications is the concentration of ownership of resources in the hands of the Scottish state — an inevitable consequence of the accrual of the oil revenues to the sovereign authority. Since I presume that all but a few diehard Stalinists would agree that concentration of the ownership of assets in the hands of the state is a dangerous thing, steps would have to be taken to see that the ownership of these resources was ultimately dispersed throughout the community. Although the sum of £1 billion could fairly quickly be used up through the purchase of existing assets in Scotland which are in non-Scottish hands, there is the additional possibility of purchasing real assets outside Scotland. Despite the Arab governments' willingness to invest abroad their surplus oil revenues, I think that foreign investment should be undertaken with extreme caution because of the danger of expropriation in the current climate of opinion which is hostile to foreign investment. It has been assumed in this paragraph that the sellers are willing to accept payment in sterling for their assets.

The remaining portion of the sterling account could in principle be devoted to (c), loans from the Scottish to the English government. The terms and conditions of these loans would of course be subject to negotiation, and the demand would vary according to conditions in the English economy. It is most unlikely that the sum required would be sufficient to use up the remaining available portion of the funds. What is left would therefore have to be invested abroad, loaned to international agencies such as the World Bank, or used for the purchase of capital goods and current goods and services outside England. Or it could simply be given away free as foreign aid. On the other hand, one could regard any unused funds as indicative of excess oil production. If the rate of production were reduced, then the oil would be left in the ground rather than transformed into a different form of capital stock.

There is an alternative solution, not man-made but accidental, to the apparent conflict of interest between Scotland and England. If significant reserves of oil, easily accessible, were discovered within English offshore waters, or large deposits of low-cost coal on land, then this would be the most desirable outcome of all.

1   Of course, it would not be expected to convert these sterling holdings into dollars. To do this, would be to negate the purpose of the scheme.

HEALTH

David Hamilton

If there is one thing that Scotland would do well at it would be the delivery of health care. Such is the strength of our Scottish tradition in medicine, that the imminent responsibility for running our own affairs makes the prospect of designing a Scottish Health Service exciting. Before discussing the possibilities presenting themselves, the present organisation and state of Scottish health will be outlined.

Health and Health Care in Scotland

The Secretary of State for Scotland is nominally in political charge of our Health Service but the Minister of Health in the Westminster Government is in practice the political chief. On the administrative side, there is devolution already to the Scottish Home and Health Department in Edinburgh.

After the introduction of the United Kingdom National Health Service in 1948 the hospitals, general practice and local authority services were separately administered, but in 1974 were reorganised into a unified administration. Local organisation of the Health Service is by district, usually containing one general hospital (called a "unit" in the new harsh terminology) and groups of districts are combined into Area Health Boards, which in turn are subordinate to the Scottish Home and Health Department. There is only a small private sector in Scotland consisting of pay beds and private clinics and a small number of part-time consultants.

The health of the Scottish nation judged by almost any standard is poorer than that of England and Wales and that of many comparable European countries, particularly the small northern democracies with whom we feel a natural affinity. The infant mortality rate (I.M.R.) is agreed to be a sensitive index of overall health and the following table shows comparisons in 1973 within the United Kingdom and internationally:[1,2]

Sweden	11	France	16	W. Germany	23
Holland	11	*England and Wales*	17	U.S.S.R.	24
Finland	11	E. Germany	18	Greece	27
Japan	12	United States	18	Poland	28
Norway	13	*Scotland*	19	Hungary	33
Denmark	14	Eire	20	Romania	42
Switzerland	14	Czechoslovakia	22	Portugal	50

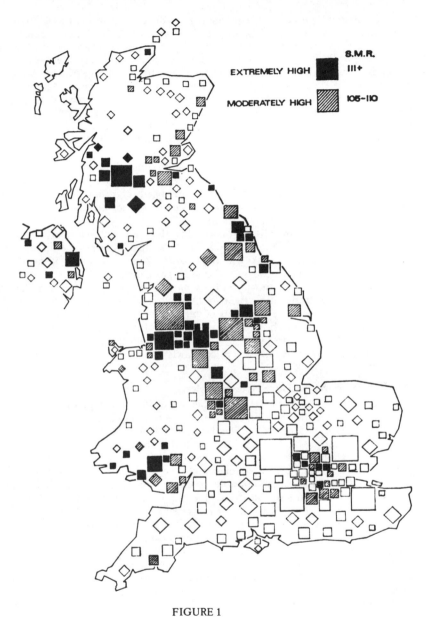

FIGURE 1
Standardised mortality rates in Britain, 1959-1963. The size of the (urban) squares and (rural) diamonds, and the distortion of the map relate to the population at risk.

From G. M. Howe: *Man, Environment and Disease in Britain.* Newton Abbot, David and
Charles, 1972.

The overall Scottish figure conceals gross differences in the I.M.R. by social class, that of Social Class I being 11.8 and that of Social Class V being 32.2: Social Class I's mortality in Scotland is equal to Social Class III in England. This factor of three in Scotland between the highest and lowest social classes has regrettably been unchanged since 1942, suggesting that the Welfare State has not yet reached, or been used, by those particularly in need. Although the I.M.R. in Scotland is declining, the rate of decline has been slower than in many European countries and whereas Scotland in 1950 occupied seventh place in the European table of Infant Mortality Rates, it now lies tenth. Indeed, there is a possibility that the I.M.R. in Scotland in 1975 for the first time will not have shown an improvement on the previous year.

As to other indexes of health, Scotland has an unequal share of the "disadvantaged" children in Britain[3] and these children are shorter, more prone to infectious disease, are less often immunised and have poorer hearing. Interestingly enough, their visual accuity (a faculty not affected by an adverse environment) is similar to other children.

Even the overall mortality in Scotland is high and contrasts sharply with the relative health of S.E. England (Fig. 1). Not only industrial Scotland has a dismal record: Scotland has the only *rural* areas of marked ill-health. In Scotland, and elsewhere, poverty and disease gang thegither.[4]

Scotland is also the most toothless nation in the civilised world, has the highest death rate from lung cancer in Europe, and is second only to Finland in coronary artery disease.[1] The effects of the abuse of alcohol and cigarettes are at their highest in Scotland, leading not only to lung cancer but also chronic bronchitis and premature birth, not only to alcoholism but also the side-effects of alcohol abuse — head injuries, falls, brawls, burns and major accidents in the home and on the road.

The Politics of the National Health Service

The birth of the National Health Service in 1948 was a political triumph for the Left and since then the National Health Service organisation and philosophy has been largely untouched. The National Health Service was a staggering advance in social justice, immediately achieving the object of making health care available freely to those in need. Its salary structures, giving identical salaries to health-care workers in any speciality or geographical area made staffing of remote districts and unfashionable specialties easy, a problem found to be almost insoluble in other countries. The National Health Service is free of the abuses seen in privately run health-care systems such as in the United States, for example, in unnecessary surgery.[5] The National Health Service has since 1948 received constant international attention because its simplicity, effectiveness and economy make it attractive to politicians and the consumer. Its reputation has been marred by periodic revolts among the medical staff, almost invariably over problems of pay. Unfortunately, the alleged misery of the National Health Service staff has been used by doctors in other countries to thwart local attempts to introduce "socialised medicine". Other current problems of the National Health Service are an acknowledged lack of humanity when dealing with individual patients, the ageing hospital buildings, the staff shortages, and delays in treatment for chronic illness. The National Health Service is seen at its best in dealing with serious or urgent disease and at its worst in dealing humanely with chronic disease.

Sadly, the National Health Service which pioneered the centrally directed type of health service, has lost the initiative in many matters of health care, and we have now to look to the small public sector in the U.S.A. for cost and quality control in health care (the medical audit) and to poor countries for the intelligent use of medical auxiliaries.[6]

Major Choices for a Scottish Health Service

Three questions must be answered at the outset in designing a Scottish Health Service. Firstly, what *kind* of service should be instituted? It would be unthinkable to return to a purely "private practice" type of health service and even the U.S.A. is rapidly moving away from this system of health care. It is a costly and ineffective service, since in spite of spending three times the amount *per capita* in the United States compared with Britain, all measurable indexes of health such as I.M.R., show no superiority to United Kingdom figures (see above). The well-off town dweller is looked after skilfully; the rural poor suffer. It also fails to provide capital for large building projects as the decaying private hospitals in the U.S.A. are well aware of.

Canada uses a second type of system where a compulsory health insurance run by government refunds to doctors and hospitals the cost of each item of treatment given to patients. This system has the advantage of allowing access by all patients equally to health care but it is more costly to run than the National Health Service since a huge administrative staff is required to operate it. The alarming increase in expenditure is causing concern, even in Canada.

The fact remains that the National Health Service remains the most economical and socially just system yet devised to provide health care for a nation. The majority of health-care workers in Scotland, all of the Scottish politicians and all of the Scottish patients would wish the present system of health care to continue, though occasionally small groups of doctors not unnaturally express their wishes for the greater rewards and freedom of the health-care systems in other countries. How far a Scottish government might go financially to dull this emigratory zeal is debatable, and the growing attraction of salaries and prospects in the E.E.C. must be recognised.[7]

Having decided on the system to be run, the next political question is the *amount* of Government expenditure that can be devoted to health. It is customary here to make international comparisons using the percentage of the G.N.P. spent to show that Britain lags behind most countries[8] but these figures conceal the actual expenditure and make no allowance for the *effectiveness* of the money spent. As noted above, the gigantic expenditure in America produces an unimpressive health record. Nor, of course, should it be presumed that pouring more national resources into the Scottish Ministry of Health will buy substantially better health, since money spent by other Ministries, such as Housing, might go further in the relief of social deprivation and consequent improvement of health, though proof of this is lacking. A socially directed health service might also achieve this.[9] Thus, one could expect the politicians responsible for Health to make a case for increased expenditure to meet the massive health problems in Scotland, bearing in mind that this must be at the relative expense of other Ministries. All functions of Government, however, might share an increase in expenditure if the present expectations of the exploitation of our natural wealth are realised.

The last question to be asked (having decided on the system of delivery and the amount to be spent) would be the *best way* of buying health within this budget. This desire for *effectiveness* will be the obsession of health-care thinkers and planners to the end of the century as will be the drive for efficiency (eg maximum use of hospital beds). Since the demand for health care is apparently limitless, priorities must be established. It is commonly assumed that the National Health Service has met every demand for health-care expenditure so far, but rationing of resources operates already, albeit in a haphazard way, since those who shout the loudest (usually aggressive doctors in expanding specialities) get the most and those without an effective lobby are denied.[11] Our health service can do better than this and indeed it is to Britain and Scotland that other countries, particularly those of the Third World, will look to a rational establishment of priorities. Only a centrally financed health service can cope with the money-eating monster that modern medicine is creating. The choices of expenditure priorities are of the following type: should the money be spent on high cost hospital medical management such as intensive care or dialysis, or should the money be spent on inexpensive help and care in the community for the elderly patients? Should the money be spent on preventive medicine such as early screening and routine check-ups in the hope of reducing ultimately the disease load, or in convalescent homes to ease the burden of chronic illness in "acute" bed hospitals? Since surgery for cancer of the lung, oesophagus, stomach and pancreas are almost ineffective, should they be abandoned? Confusion in the Health Service among doctors and administrators about its ultimate role is almost total and explains the astonishing receptiveness to new ideas by the profession. Ivan Illich's frontal attack on the health profession[10], in which he boldly stated that the net contribution of doctors to health was not only zero but may be less than nothing and argued that since modern medicine is organised to give expensive, dangerous treatment to a few it denies simple help and care to the rest, had sympathetic reviews in the *British Medical Journal*.

Even the choices given above may be misleading and cause further troubles. Money put into geriatrics may help the comfort of the aged, but as life expectancy at age 65 has been unchanged for many decades, more money is unlikely to prolong life. Simply to ban renal dialysis might save money, but would result in a public outcry and the emergence of a particularly unjust private sector. Indeed the Left have suggested a ban on the private sector[12] to allow central priorities to be established. Even this would not thwart communities sending patients abroad for treatment. Lastly, the attraction of prevention and early diagnosis may be illusory, or ultimately costly. The value of early diagnosis of breast cancer is dubious; early detection of phenylketonuria prevents brain damage, but gives a huge annual bill to the nation for the special diet required.

As Professor Sam Galbraith has stated many times, society must decide whether to treat individuals or groups.

It would be an enormous step forward if we even knew in the Scottish Health Service how much each individual treatment cost, the number of lives saved and even the improvement in each patient on a simple index of health. Thus the kidney dialysis unit often singled out for criticism because of the high cost, would come out fairly well since they restore to a reasonably quality of life young people who would otherwise be dead, something that cannot be said for the treatment of many cancers. Coronary care units might come off less well as their value is debatable in terms of clinical benefit and when this is divided by the cost, would be less attractive. The modern obstetric hospital where colossal expenditure is required to anticipate occasional complications of the natural process of childbirth would also be low on the cost-effectiveness scale.

The key problems therefore to be coped with in a future Scottish Health Service are those which will inevitably occur in all nations because of the nature of medical progress. There is almost a limitless potential for expenditure. Only a health service refunded by central Government can deal with this problem and in Scotland we are well placed to do so.

Relationship between Government and Health Care Workers

In 1948 the relationship between the two was simple. Government paid the salaries and modest bills and the doctors got on with the healing of the sick. As newer forms of therapy were discovered, the National Health Service would stump up, not only for new forms of expensive therapy, but for new kinds of organisations such as screening clinics and new kinds of health-care workers such as ward receptionists and community physicians. Central Government itself gradually took on the task of deciding on its allocation of money while the profession themselves stood back from decision-making and grumbled about their pay. Examples of the lack of debate and accountability are not hard to find. A massive cut-back in the hospital building programme was intimated first to a private meeting of the tiny Medical Practitioners Union, only then slowly reaching the medical press.[13]

Much of the unhappiness of the profession is its subservient role to the Government and civil servants. If some degree of responsibility could be returned to the doctors in the Scottish Health Service, then the Scottish doctors might rise to the challenges of the future. Indeed there is almost no other way that the inevitable limitations on the kind of medicine possible will be achieved than by a partnership between Government and the health workers with mutual respect and appreciation of the other's problems.

A Health Commission

"If the National Health Service is to be strengthened, we must find a way of entering into a new, less bitter dialogue between the medical profession and Government. For if the suspicions and the resentments could only be broken down, the medical profession could find it would play a great constructive part with Government."[14]

To create a partnership we require a new institution which we could call a Health Commission. It would be responsible for the running of the Health Service in Scotland. It would be analogous to the type of body already running other nationalised industries such as British Airways, Rail and Steel. The Commission should be chaired by a Moderator (the term Health Commissioner having been pre-empted by the Ombudsman) appointed for a fixed period of time, say seven years, thus giving a measure of stability. This period would be two or three times greater than the average tenure of office of recent Ministers of Health. The Commission would be elected in part by the doctors, dentists and all other health-care workers, and by Government, and would be supported by the Civil Service, at present running the Health Service. The commission would continue and strengthen the "consumer-orientated" research programme run by the Chief Scientist. The Commission's deliberations would be made more public and decision-making in health care would at last be more open and decisions made would be attributable. The role of the Minister of Health in day-to-day decision-making would thus be deliberately diminished.

However, the political process must be maintained and major medical political issues included in election manifestos and subsequently approved by Parliament, would be sent by the Minister to the Moderator for implementation. Although contentious health-care issues (such as pay beds in 1975 and prescription charges in the 1960's) gain prominence from time to time, they are in fact rare and hence confrontation of Government and the Commission is unlikely.

Below the Commission, the bureaucratic organisation of medicine brought about by the recent reorganisation is universally disliked and has greatly increased the number of administrators. By abolition of one tier of administration (the most obvious target being the Area Health Boards) this can be reversed at a stroke. Thus in Glasgow, the Greater Glasgow Health Board will go (as must the Strathclyde Region) and no tears would be shed for either. This attack on bureaucracy is a theme running through the S.N.P. manifesto.

At the hospital and health centre level the Scottish health-care workers are more receptive to ideas of hospital democracy, in which the élite groups must eventually co-operate with all other groups and recognise that all have a part to play.

An Academy of Medicine

To assist the Health Commission, the health-care workers must be better organised, both for representation on clinical matters and for trade union purposes. The regulation and representation of the doctors in particular is at present done in bits and pieces by various bodies, none of which can be said to be representative of the profession, nor to speak for all of them. The B.M.A. has been slow to take up any causes other than financial ones and their present declining membership, lack of grass-roots support and right-wing views must cause concern. The colleges in Scotland have an international reputation but have traditionally stood apart from matters other than clinical ones. Even when one college speaks out (e.g. the London College of Physicians' Report on Flouridation) its views lack the backing of the whole profession, and hence carry less weight. Interestingly enough, in recent years the colleges have sensed the lack of political representation of the profession and have increasingly volunteered opinions on health-care matters beyond their remit. This makes the idea of an all-embracing organisation for doctors in Scotland (which might be called an Academy of Medicine) an attractive one. The membership could be compulsory with part of the fee going to the appropriate specialist college (thus securing their position), another fraction being used for the functions previously carried out by the General Medical Council, and the rest for the trade union activities of the B.M.A. The Academy's committees could supervise the growing field of post-graduate education and the increasingly important work of speciality education and registration. The strength of the Academy would also enable observation of changes abroad and negotiation with our European partners in the E.E.C. The views of the Academy would be authoritative and would be respected by the Health Commission and the commission would be wise to remit the inevitable problem of measuring the quality and efficiency of medical care by individual doctors, the "medical audit" to the Academy.

The Patient and the Scottish Health Service

The Scottish Health Service must ultimately exist for the people of Scotland in health and disease. People require three things of a Health Service — *choice, representation* and *accountability*. The patient must have freedom to choose his medical advisers, thus maintaining confidence on the patient's side and standards on the doctor's. Though choice is currently thought to be the strong point of the private sector, in fact mechanisms exist within the Health Service for choice, both of a G.P. and consultant and for obtaining a "second opinion". These opportunities need only be pointed out and strengthened. Secondly, the patient requires representation in the organisation of health care in their district. The new Community Councils, on paper, fulfil this role but their nominated (rather than elected) composition is a source of weakness and must prevent any real crusader gaining membership. It is however too early to assess their effect. The new Health Commissioner (an ombudsman equivalent) can investigate complaints of administrative delays and inhumanity of management and his first report shows how common these can be. His report[15] has already produced helpful reaction in the National Health Service. Lastly, the profession must be ultimately accountable for its standard of treatment to any individual patient. The "mystique" of the medical profession must surely be shed ultimately, allowing the community more knowledge of health care and making the doctor more approachable. As to standards, it would be thought that the law courts provide sufficient recourse for the latter complaints, though there is evidence that this is no longer a satisfactory solution. Many of the so-called "medico-legal" incidents are not compensated because the patient has to initiate unpleasant and expensive legal proceedings to obtain even an *ex gratia* payment, and the medical, dental and nursing professions themselves, faced with the possible stigma of negligence, are instructed never to admit to any shortcomings of management. Only when compensation can be removed from the need to prove negligence can just and fair arrangements be made for patients suffering as a result of treatment. Moreover, as medicine becomes increasingly sophisticated, the side-effects of treatment, though rare, become more serious. Thus, a patient damaged from a drug side-effect or a rare complication of surgery or an X-ray may not be compensated at all (with rare exceptions[16]) and they may be worse off from the colossal legal fees involved in bringing the matter to judgment. Paradoxically, an honest citizen assaulted in the street and left with a similar incapacity will be compensated by the Criminal Injuries Board. No compensation is given to a patient contracting hepatitis from a blood transfusion or a needle prick, but a doctor or technician similarly infected at work will be compensated by the Industrial Injuries Board. The concept of a "no blame" compensation[17] would be one which a modern Health Service would do well to think about. Its humanity is reachable and it would moreover prevent the growth of the extraordinary medical litigation in the United States[18] and all the perversions of health care and legal practice which it produces.

General Practice

From being the most discontented section in the Health Service, general practice is now noticeably more self-assured and has recently been strengthened, both financially and professionally. Higher levels of remuneration, addition of elementary financial incentives, the growth of health centres with their provision of support by district nurses and other para-medical workers (constituting the so-called "primary health-care team") have given a more satisfactory professional life for the practitioner. It has, moreover, strengthened the most cost-effective part of health care, since it deals with 90% of the contacts between patient and doctor yet costs 8% of the National Budget. This effectiveness of primary health care in Britain is admired internationally. Nevertheless the load of trivial illness by-passing the G.P. and being dealt with at outpatient and casualty departments is substantial and can be reduced further by better primary health care. Primary health care itself can be reduced by more "self help".[19] The special problems of health care in remote areas in Scotland must also be safeguarded, in spite of high cost, and the quality of service and health care in these areas is recognised. The temptation to over-centralise the present rural hospital facilities should be resisted, since though they may be costly, the effectiveness of care and efficiency of follow-up is higher than in the city. Moreover, the removal of these small hospitals would lead to loss of confidence in the community and a considerable financial burden to patients and their relatives in travel to distant hospitals. It is to be anticipated, moreover, that the population of the Highlands will grow.

Private Sector

The private sector in Scotland differs from that in England in a number of ways. First of all it is very small, as is the number of private practitioners. The average consultant in Scotland is not enthusiastic about private practice and trainees are often actively hostile to it. It was not surprising therefore that during the English industrial action to support private practice, the Scots declined to join it. Pay beds in the hospitals make the majority of staff (medical and non-medical) uncomfortable, but some privacy should be able to be purchased on the Scottish Health Service — the so-called "amenity" bed should be made available again. The phasing out of pay beds should therefore be supported in Scotland but a free society cannot abolish the private sector completely. However, the private sector's nursing care and the availability of medical help and equipment in emergencies, must be up to standard to protect the private patient. If the hospital building programme in the National Health Service can be completed and waiting-lists reduced, then the private sector will disappear.

National Health Service as an Economic Force

The economic effects of the spending of the National Health Service budget has received little attention.[20] In Scotland an annual budget of £100m. is available to be spent on drugs and simple consumable items such as butter, jam, uniforms, crockery, fuel, drugs, syringes and needles, plus a larger sum for substantial equipment and new hospital buildings. There is every evidence that these considerable sums are spent largely outside Scotland, the orders being placed with large firms able to meet the bulk orders and competitive specifications and who alone are able to shave the cost to the minimum. The result is that in Scotland we have hardly any industry supplying consumables for the National Health Service nor do we have any pharmaceutical industry. The Scottish Government would be wise to use the budget of the Scottish Health Service (and indeed of all nationalised industries) as a stimulus to industry in

Scotland by the simple expedient of ordering supplies locally, a philosophy already accepted in the oil-related industries.

Since no pharamaceutical industry exists in Scotland, it might be an opportunity to examine closely the strengths and defects of this industry. Its undoubted strength is its good record in the introduction of new drugs, which largely come from this industry rather than basic science laboratories. Its major weakness is the huge spending of money on promotion of drugs, often of old drugs or combinations of familiar drugs under new names. A Scottish Government would have control of the drug industry via the Scottish Health Service and in legislating for a pharmaceutical presence in Scotland, we would have a range of choices between, on the one hand, allowing a totally free-enterprise pharmaceutical industry and on the other, the radical option chosen in Allende's Chile of restricting the pharmacopoeia to five drugs of proven value provided as plain white tablets and manufactured in government factories.[21] An industry which has ignored, and hence impoverished, Scotland heretofore cannot escape critical examination.

Manpower Resources and Career Prospects

A manpower crisis in the United Kingdom is anticipated shortly, resulting from the chronic under-production of United Kingdom doctors, continued emigration by them to other countries and the recent cut-off of our supply of foreign doctors from Africa and India to the United Kingdom after higher standards have been demanded by the General Medical Council. Scotland will survive this crisis better than England and Wales, since our traditionally high output of medical students will continue. Happily, applicants to do medicine in Scotland have not been discouraged by the present difficulties in the Health Service and the Medical Faculties in Scotland continue to attract the best qualified school-leavers. An independent Scottish Health Service would be well placed to examine and reverse the traditional emigration of Scottish health-care workers. The National Health Service makes poor use of the large number of women doctors (a number which will increase as university applicants now have to be considered on merit and without regard to their sex). Novel forms of contract, and conditions of work, allowing for full home and family life, must be experimented with.

The nursing profession in Scotland is surviving the present shortages better than in England but is burdened with a widely criticised top-heavy bureaucratic career structure which removes talented nurses from the wards into the administration, a move often forced only by better salaries. It is essential to encourage a continuation of a clinical career for nurses by giving comparable salaries in these jobs.

Relationship with Other Countries

Internationalism has always been a feature of Scottish medicine and Scottish doctors and nurses were found throughout the world often in situations where they were most needed and least rewarded. The National Health Service in recent years has stifled this internationalism making no positive provision for it, and the rigid career structures make it increasingly difficult to arrange leave of absence to help for short periods in developing countries. Ironically, the National Health Service also removes graduates from underdeveloped countries

73

desperately short of doctors and uses them to staff our health services, often placing them in unattractive posts without prospect of education or promotion, and in which they are secretly derided. This affront to Scottish hospitality must cease and visitors incorporated into proper training schemes, suitable to their needs.

A Scottish Government would discuss with the developing countries their manpower problems and take steps, not only to help but also to prevent making these worse. We can also help by extending the expertise of the Scottish Health Service to other countries. The days of the medical missionary, in which Scotland played an honourable part, may be drawing to a close, but new forms of help are required in these countries — short-term appointments, specialist training for short periods in Scotland, administrative help, assistance after natural disasters, and help with hospital building design and construction.

Health Education and Legislation

A substantial part of the budget of Scottish health is spent on illnesses which are self-inflicted. Identifiable damage is done by smoking, drinking, driving cars and eating sweets. Outright abolition of all these by Government action would give a healthier community and reduce the health-care budget, but action of this kind would be seen as an intolerable intrusion into personal freedom. Hence action of this nature is unattainable at present under our democratic process, though if the citizen allows the Government to increase his freedom from disease, then Government can be allowed to reduce his freedom of action to injure himself. A policy of eventual elimination through gradual legislation and education can, therefore, be adopted. The successful introduction of seat-belt legislation, a measure designed only to protect the individual from himself, is a case in point. Outright banning of cars is unthinkable but an overall speed limit of 40-50 miles an hour is not. Sweets could easily be banned, leading to increased dental health but the problems of the abuse of alcohol and cigarettes provide a much more insuperable task. Systematically increasing the tax on cigarettes (perhaps annually) together with health education, seems to be winning that battle in Norway, but no country in the world has yet made any impact on alcoholism. Seductive advertising of cigarettes and alcohol must eventually cease. One hopes, like the Clayson Committee, that liberalisation of the licensing laws in Scotland will produce healthier attitudes to drinking. A reduction in social deprivation might also help. This, however, remains an expression of faith.

Finally . . .

The opportunity to run a Scottish Health Service may soon exist. Many of the ideas discussed above can be implemented even by a minimally devolved Scottish Assembly. The basic design of the National Health Service will remain as it is the one wanted by patients and its structure is the most economical to run. Scotland is particularly well placed now to deal with the many defects which frustrate the functioning of the National Health Service in Britain and blur its reputation abroad. Government and the profession in Scotland must enter into a partnership if the Health Service is to advance and deal with the coming crisis of manpower and resources. The prospects of success in Scotland are good. For encouragement in this task, we can turn to Lord Boyd Orr's views on Scotland,[22] himself Scotland's most eminent medical graduate, a great internationalist and a devoted nationalist — "We have the men, we have the materials: all we need is a touch of ancient fire in our hearts".

1 "Health Services in Scotland Report for 1974", H.M.S.O., Edinburgh.
2 "Annual Report of the Chief Medical Officer, 1972-73", H.M.S.O., London.
3 P. Wedge and H. Prosser: *Born to Fail*, Arrow Books, 1973.
4 Political use of health statistics is not new. In a famous incident, Jimmy Maxton (I.L.P.) was suspended from the House of Commons after describing as "murderers" Government Ministers who proposed withdrawing the supply of free milk from poor mothers and children, thus raising the I.M.R. (*Hansard* 165, C. 2379).
5 C. E. Lewis: *New England Journal of Medicine*, 1969, 281, p. 880.
6 In Bangladesh, auxiliaries trained in one surgical procedure (tubal ligation) proved as good as trained personnel. *Lancet*, ii, 1975, p. 568.
7 Net earnings for G.P.s in the E.E.C. are usually £12,000. Specialists are fully trained after five years and can earn a gross £30,000 in many of these countries, compared with a maximum of £10,700 in the United Kingdom. *British Medical Journal*, i, 1976, p. 139.
8 The United Kingdom spends 5.2% of G.N.P. on health, "less than any country at a comparable state of development". G. Forsyth in "Health Service Prospects", *Nuffield Provincial Hospitals Trust*, 1973, p. 9.
9 Sir John Brotherston: *Lancet*, ii, 1975, p. 667.
10 I. Illich: *Medical Nemesis*, Calder and Boyers, 1974.
11 Even so, the National Health Service is near crisis point. The £2m. required for therapy of haemophiliacs was the subject of public debate: if the new operations for narrowing of the coronary arteries had been as effective as hoped, massive numbers of surgeons would have had to be trained for it; if every pregnant woman demanded the examination of the foetus for Mongolism, further costly resources would have to be provided.
12 Donald Gould in *New Statesman*, 21st November 1975.
13 Editorial, *Lancet*, ii, 1975, p. 1248.
14 Mrs B. Castle, Nye Bevan Memorial Lecture. Quoted in *New Statesman*, 2nd January 1976.
15 "First Report of the Health Commissioner, 1974-5", H.M.S.O., London.
16 Children with brain damage after whooping-cough vaccination now receive compensation from the Government, *Sunday Times*, 22nd September 1974. After a monumental struggle the Thalidomide-damaged children were given an *ex gratia* payment by the Distillers Company.
17 *British Medical Journal*, iii, 1975, p. 529
18 Awards recently of over $1m. have been made in California almost at a rate of one a month. New York orthopaedic surgeons' insurance premiums are $60,000 a year. The rate is £20 in Scotland. *British Journal of Hospital Medicine*, March 1975, p. 385.
19 P. Pigache: "World Medicine", 9th April 1975, records a bold attempt to educate a community to look after simple illness. This movement is being neutralised by the "consult your doctor for any abnormality" propaganda, particularly from the early diagnosis of cancer enthusiasts.
20 "The power and the patronage of the public sector now exceeds the power and patronage of the private sector." Isobel Lindsay, *Scots Independent*, June 1975.
21 H. Waitzken and H. Modell: *New England Journal of Medicine*, 291, 1974, p. 171-177.
22 Lord Boyd Orr: *The Scotland of our Sons*, Maclehose, Glasgow, 1937, p. 109.

F

HOUSING

Colin Bell

Despite the endless assurances in both Labour and Conservative programmes for more than half a century, Scotland still has a housing problem. Indeed, it is a problem not only in itself, but one which lies at the root of many others — education, employment, health, crime, depopulation, and, through its pressure on local authority spending and borrowing, has contributed to slumpflation too.

The solutions offered, and even tried, by the established Unionist parties have plainly failed to work. There should be no surprise at this; for their palliatives have been grounded in rival ideologies which have seen housing as a weapon, or a burden, and not for what it is — the provision of homes. But if their policies have been distorted by political consideration, so has their analysis of the problem. Scotland has been led to believe that the housing problem is one of shortage, pure and simple, and that mere numbers will supply the answer.

This is simply not the case. Scotland's housing problem is not so much one of insufficient dwellings, but of inadequate dwellings, and dwellings in the wrong places. We should be building more, far more, homes; but the demand that must be met is not one for endless new dwellings built to already outdated and skimpy standards, on ghetto estates, in west central Scotland, but for homes of a much higher standard, and offering much greater flexibility of choice and richness of environment, in those areas where houses will either meet an existing need generated by industrial and other economic development, or where their provision will facilitate such development in the future — or where they will infuse new life into existing communities. There can be no development, no expansion, no vigour for the future, without adequate housing. If we seek to encourage, as we must, labour mobility, and wish to revivify depressed areas, we must have better homes, in better settings.

Political Prejudices of Labour and Conservatives

Mere quantity has dominated the approach of the Labour and Conservative Parties, and political prejudice has dictated their chosen methods. The Labour Party's idealists have persisted in the belief that housing is a social service — and that it must therefore be provided by orthodox social means: built, owned and managed by public authorities, Labour's cynics have grown to think that this monopoly of housing supply offers the perfect method of attracting, disciplining, and regimenting a solid Labour vote. Housing policy has become a form of gerrymandering.

The Tories ideological commitment has been to private ownership, and their electoral debt has been to those who see the council tenant as a shiftless, ever-subsidised burden on the backs of the ratepayers and the taxpayers.

Housing is of course a social service. And our present dependence on public authority housing represents a burden on society at large.

76

Housing is a social service immediately we assent to the proposition that we should not let anybody go unhoused. It does not matter if we accept the responsibility to house just one impoverished family, or everyone; once it is understood that the homeless ought to be sheltered, then we have implicitly committed ourselves to providing universal shelter. The problem is therefore one of method, not of principle. How best can society house itself?

Labour's customary answer seems to have failed. The consequence of placing the responsibility on local and national government has been to minimise housing standards, minimise housing life, and maximise the housing debt, which bears so heavily on the authorities with the greatest demand that they are quite unable to cope with the other social expenditure made necessary by the poor quality of their individual homes and general housing environments. It is quite apparent that a generation of local authority housing effort in Glasgow has not only failed to solve the "housing problem", but has contributed to the growth of all sorts of other social problems. A new Easterhouse might be built every year, and still Glasgow's urban deprivation would top the Northern European table; it would indeed grow relatively worse, since standards are constantly rising elsewhere in the world.

Scotland has long been a relatively poor country. Labour has been committed not only to public provision of housing, but to low rents. In their turn, the Conservatives have pined for higher rents, but often lacked the power, or the conviction, to make them stick. The housing authorities have therefore exacerbated their already shaky finances by receiving income which only rarely services the enormous capital debt. Housing standards have reflected this constant threat of bankruptcy, and the greater part of the people's contribution to the housing account has flowed south to pay off interest.

Scotland has been starved of capital; but our collective income has been cruelly taxed to finance borrowing, and we have failed to spend enough of our individual incomes on housing anyway. The proportion of our disposable incomes that we spend on housing is significantly lower than in most other comparable countries; and the result, encouraged as it has been by the Labour Party, is that our housing standards are lower too, and that we have to be taxed in other ways to help offset the housing costs.

Oil: a panacea?

It would be quite foolish, and short-sighted, to cry at this point that the oil will cure our problems. The value of the oil is that it represents an opportunity to generate new skills, new productive industries, and new investment capital. Whatever the ultimate arrangement by which Scotland benefits from its own resources, it certainly cannot be seen as a cornucopia of lavish pocket-money, to be spent by one generation at the expense of the next. For a start, Scotland will only enjoy a proportion of its gross market valuation; for either we export it, and thus retain only some reasonable proportion of its value, or we consume it, in which case we are ourselves paying out that value. Its balance of payments effects will be very great, and any sensible system of ownership, or participation, of royalties and of profits taxes, will return to Scotland a handsome income. But that income should be husbanded; kept on tap for many years by proper conservation and depletion, and used, when received, for projects that will help guarantee Scotland's prosperity long after all the oil has gone. We cannot simply enter in our books the estimated gross value of the deposits, and proceed to spend against that figure on every kind of immediate consumption. That is the U.K. Treasury way — and merely staves off chaos for another decade.

In fact, in this as in so many other areas, it might be more sensible to plan for the new Scotland without counting on the oil. Of course the oil is there; and of course Scotland must get some compensation for the depletion of this national resource. But it can be very dangerous to make oil the answer to all our problems, not least because to do so may prevent us from thinking through our problems in the first place.

Solutions to the housing problem are nevertheless going to cost money; where must it come from, if not from oil? From ourselves, of course. It may well be that the wise investment of oil revenues will create work where now there is none, and will raise real incomes; we may therefore find it easier to spend more of our wages on our housing, but that is what we have to do, oil or no oil.

National Housing Stock

Let us go back to the argument about housing as a social service. If there is general agreement that everybody ought to have a home, and that it is a communal responsibility to ensure that they do, it raises two immediate questions. The first is obviously: how best can we supply homes for everyone? The second is not quite so obvious, but equally significant: is there any meaning in the idea of ownership?

If we must find a means of housing everyone who needs a home, then all housing units are part of a common national stock. If I buy my own house for my own family, then I reduce by one the number of houses which society must build collectively. What I have bought, and ultimately caused to be built, is a house; when I move, or die, the community still has a house, into which someone else may move. For the moment, we must forget the monetary value of that house, and the notion that I somehow own it much as a capitalist may own a factory, or as I indubitably own my furniture.

For owner-occupied homes are not means of production, nor are they portable wealth. They are part of the national fund of homes just as much as are those "owned" by the S.S.H.A., or by a local authority or a public corporation. They do of course rise in value in certain circumstances, so that the money that the owner has paid proves to have been an investment, insofar as he receives on sale more than he paid out on purchase. But even if the original purchase, through a mortgage or other loan, has enjoyed favourable tax concessions, this does not affect the status of the house as a house. Obviously, it is open to any Government to treat realised profit as taxable, and apply some form of gains, or capital transfer, or estate taxation to the enhanced value of a house. But the real social concern must be with housing, more than with fears that some lucky house-buyer is going to make a killing with the Revenue's help. The morality of private ownership should be judged by what it does for the housing stock, not by what it does for the occasional private owner.

The peculiar nature of wealth when locked up in a family's first or only home quite distinguishes it from the generality of private property. Indeed, this is officially recognised in such nominally socialist economies as Romania, where it is the citizen's duty to aspire to home-ownership, and thus spare the State the cost of housing him. In the U.K. at large the average mortgage is redeemed after about seven or eight years. This does not represent a mass of tax-pampered profiteers taking their money and running; it is the normal mobility of life. Jobs change, families are founded, grow, and shrink again, aspirations vary; so house-owner X sells his only house, and buys another. His house in turn may now be bought by Y, who has sold his house, or has embarked on his first purchase. There will be very little loose cash spilling around on this housing chain, which can very often stretch away to involve a score or more of families. The two socially desirable objectives must surely be to see that the friction loss (to agents, solicitors, advertising, mortgage holders, etc.) should be kept to a minimum, since this takes money out of the housing chain, and to see that at some stage the profits generated end up as the finance for new housing. Profits taken, and clearly bound for the likes of the Cayman Islands, could be taxed at penal rates; profits which are merely reapplied to buying housing are scarcely wealth at all.

The objective is to expand and improve the housing stock, not to enforce equality. Egalitarian social policies may be pursued by means which do not enforce immobility, and means which do not discourage socially desirable investment — and building houses out of voluntary private savings must surely be such an investment.

The Myth of Private Ownership

The advantages of the myth of private ownership do not lie entirely in its ability to mobilise private savings, and private borrowing, to take the burden of housing off the community at large. It is a very powerful myth, for there is now overwhelming evidence that homes nominally owned by their occupants are kept in better maintenance, are more frequently improved, and generally last much longer, than do homes nominally owned and actually managed by public authorities. In London, Liverpool, Middlesbrough, Dundee, Glasgow, Paisley and Alloa, to cite only the best-known examples, there are post-war estates which have already fallen into ruin, and are scheduled for demolition. What this means is that homes built on money borrowed over 30, 40, even 60 years, have become slums long before their capital cost has been repaid.

And the attractions of ownership, as every political party recognises with more or less frankness, appeal to a very large proportion of those at present paying rents to public housing authorities. Tenants do want to buy their own homes; and only a stubborn commitment by the Labour Party to an outmoded doctrine prevents us from mobilising that reserve of enthusiasm. It is socially wasteful to deny a tenant the right to assume all the responsibility for his home, just as it would be socially unjust to place such stress on the alleged moral superiority of owner-occupation that we left only the very worst public housing available for those who prefer to rent. The solution must be to ration the sale of our present public stock in proportion to the flow of new homes into the stock, so that there will always be decent homes to rent, and always opportunities to convert from renting to buying.

Demand-Management

Regulating the flow of houses is central to the entire problem. It is very unlikely that we shall, in our lifetime, have to worry about means of restricting supply, and the concern is therefore with increasing it, and with keeping it in equilibrium with the pace and pattern of demand. At present, in both private and public sectors, demand is expressed almost exclusively in money terms; the tap is not one of housing need, but of macro-economic circumstances. Here again, the great challenge for the new Scotland is to remove housing from the vagaries of the business cycle, and of demand-management tinkering.

The traditional situation is that in times of general boom, the construction industry gears itself up, receives orders from public authorities, and perceives that the demand from the private sector will repay the cost of financing speculative building. Because of the lags inherent in the industry — finding land, getting planning consent, competing for the resources of money, material, plant and labour — this building boom starts late, and generates cost inflation. Because it has started late, purchasers have found their confidence, and their finance, before the flow of new homes has risen, and this generates existing-house price inflation. In the boom of the early 1970's, the costs of land, of building materials, of labour, and of houses rose. In a situation where homes seemed a good investment, where paper profits were easily made liquid, and where mortgage finance was readily available, much money was directed not to new construction, but to a giddy process of trading up, whereby those already housed took on bigger and more expensive houses, even second homes, and the floor price for homes appealing to first-time buyers rose out of the reach of many potential purchasers.

From the public authorities' point of view, construction costs rose, debts rose, and homes only became available to rent as the capacity of some tenants to meet economic rentals began to suffer from the onset of the slump. Government interference to keep rents low meant that local authorities could only service their inflated debt by further borrowing or by Government subsidy. This too has inevitably proved inflationary, and has both increased the taxation cost of housing and reduced funds available for other social spending.

The trick is obviously to relate housing supply to housing demand, and not to any other variable. For the existing system generates enormous waste, and insufficient housing. Waste, because when skilled men are laid off, when small entrepreneurs are bankrupted, when plant is repossessed and materials are stockpiled, that is a loss which can never be replaced. We cannot add an extra year or two to the life of a joiner or a plumber or an architect to make up for the years he could not work. We cannot expand the capacity of the industry so that it can catch up on years already lost, not if the demands of the rest of the economy in the good years are to be met, and certainly not if the industry fears that slump or "stop" will soon be back again.

Waste, too, because the savings of depositors, and of borrowers, from Building Societies are merely adding to inflation in the good years, and can find no outlet in the bad. And waste because the local authorities are forced to borrow hard in the "go" years, while the public spending cuts of the bad times leave them with only one uncuttable, and unhelpful, item — servicing their housing debt.

Predicting Demand

Housing demand can be predicted fairly easily. At present, the most difficult factor in doing so is to forecast the availability of funds; for although the cost of borrowing naturally has some effect, the most significant element in the unleashing of demand is simply the ease with which money may be borrowed. Naturally, the total demand, or the social target, will vary according to the standards which consumers come to expect, or which society decides that it should set. Average occupation densities in Scotland are markedly higher than in England, Germany, Scandinavia — so that we must expect our target to change over time, as we upgrade our own expectations.

Nevertheless, a target can be arrived at without undue difficulty; and some of the variables over time can also be predicted — population changes, likely annual losses by irremediable deterioration, the upward movement of standards. This target must be related to the availability of resources, and to the optimal capacity of the industry. Perhaps the greatest single improvement that we could make would be to establish an annual target in the knowledge that it would be maintained for a number of years. Only in the security of that knowledge could we be sure of the maximum co-operation of the construction industry, who might then be confident that investment made now would not be nullified by adverse economic movement, nor by Government interference in pursuit of non-housing goals.

This plainly involves central Government in certain guarantees: it must announce a target which represents not only the collective wisdom of civil servants who have assessed long-run demand, and of the industry, which will have forecast its long-run capacity in conditions of sustained consumption, but also of politicians, who must decide what proportion of G.N.P., or inflation-proofed amount of money, will be made available, free from tinkering and regulating, each year.

The Building Societies

But these guarantees, even in a situation where central Government is either constructing houses for the public sector, or advancing mortgages for private purchase, can still not ensure a stable flow if private sources of housing finance are not regulated. The Building Society method of fostering private ownership has proved, in England, as good as any of the other private-sector methods employed in the U.S.A. in France, or in Australia; but it has not yet served Scotland quite as well, and it will require further supervision if it is not to threaten the delicate balance of a long-run housing strategy.

The most important political point is that the Societies, overwhelmingly English-based, have recently expanded into Scotland at a remarkably rapid rate. And the simplest calculations must reveal, despite the evasions, and rather unspecific denials, of the movement's spokesmen, that their present effect is to tap Scottish savings for the benefit of borrowers throughout the U.K. Since there are far fewer borrowers in Scotland, proportionately and in absolute numbers, while the average number of depositers, and amounts deposited, per Branch seem constant, this means that Scotland is experiencing a net loss of savings, and England a net gain. It is also worth remarking that the movement, which places so much emphasis on increasing branches, and on having them in prime High Street positions, demonstrates a curious immunity to the customary economies of scale: big Societies spend as large a proportion of their income on administration, premises, fixtures and fittings as do the smaller ones. Engaged as they are in quite farcical "competition" (farcical because the terms they offer to both depositor and borrower are almost indistinguishable; the only selling proposition each can offer is the number or situation of its branches), they are a peculiarly wasteful means of channeling savings into housing.

To meet these points, the new Scotland should insist that Building Societies be separately incorporated in Scotland, and that their accounts for these Scottish associates of English undertakings demonstrate quite clearly that savings deposited in Scotland are used exclusively for mortgages granted in Scotland. The U.K. average for home-ownership is about 52 per cent; since Scotland's average is only around 30 per cent, and forms part of the U.K. average, it must follow that England at present enjoys substantially more than 50 per cent home ownership. If Scotland needs, as I believe it does, to encourage far wider private ownership and co-operative ownership, it cannot afford for many years to come to lend its savings furth of Scotland, particularly at the relatively low rates offered by Building Societies. These rates are, incidentally, negative; they have not matched inflation in recent years. The willingness of savers to accept a loss over time is a godsend to the relative stability of society in the face of historically high inflation rates, but there is no need for Scotland, relatively short of domestic investment in the past, and with a huge backlog to redress in the future, to accept negative interest abroad.

This aside, the most dangerous element in the free functioning of such private sources is that their lending is geared to the flow of deposits, and not to the flow of houses. In other words, when funds are high, they will attract borrowers, regardless of the availability of new homes: and thus engender a seller's market in existing houses. This not only inflates the prices of houses which already form part of the stock, it has adverse knock-on effects. In an atmosphere of spiralling house-prices, borrowers take on debts beyond their means — for not only do they borrow on the incomes earned in relatively good times, discounting risks of unemployment, or of inflation which can rapidly increase the proportion of income necessarily spent on other essentials such as food and clothing, but when funds are high, Building Societies have tended to loosen their restrictions over such highly elastic variables as overtime earnings, wife's earnings, and required deposit ratios. Furthermore, the apparent rise in house prices encourages speculative development, driving up the price of land, of materials and labour.

Similarly, when the net inflow of lendable funds is low, the Building Societies are unable to accommodate all the willing borrowers; the housing market becomes sluggish; labour mobility is depressed, since selling proves not only difficult, but runs the risk of showing a loss; speculative builders go bankrupt, men are laid off. Local authorities may buy completed private-sector houses, which does not of course increase the stock at all, but does increase their housing debt.

Controlling Building Societies

Obviously, the problem is to integrate the Building Societies with the national housing target, and to maximise their contribution to new-house finance, rather than existing-house price inflation. If we assume that Government has set a national target for new housing, and intends to increase over time the proportion of those houses which are destined for the owner-occupier, the housing association, or the co-operative, it must also ensure that the price of houses increases at a socially acceptable target rate as well. If their price advances more slowly than general inflation, then incentive is lost; if it exceeds that rate, then the returns will generate speculative building, and the bidding-up of wage and material and land costs.

The target rate of increase can be defined, perhaps, as being equal to the rise in the Retail Price Index, thus reflecting the "normal" rate of increase of building costs, plus that amount necessary to keep pace with the rise in the relative price of land caused by the pressure of non-housing demand for land.

In order that the Building Societies should play their part in achieving the two targets — of construction and of relative price stability — they must be obliged by Government to act as follows:

1. Advances on existing properties must be increased at that rate, neither more nor less, that will cause the price of existing properties to increase at the target rate. To calculate the precise rate of increase of advances necessary to achieve this target is somewhat complex. But if we assume, for simplicity's sake, that a constant proportion of the existing housing stock comes onto the market each year, and that a constant proportion of the flow of demand for existing houses is financed by Building Society mortgages, the mandatory rate of increase of those mortgages, net of repayments, is equal to the target rate of increase of house prices plus the net percentage rate of increase in the volume of the private housing stock.

2. Similarly, advances on new properties must be made at that rate, neither more nor less, which will cause both the target rate of increase in the volume of housing and the target rate of increase in house prices to be achieved. The mandatory level of advances on new properties in any year will thus depend on the absolute size and the target rate of increase in the stock of private housing and on the absolute level and the target rate of increase of house prices. Each year, then, the level of advances on new properties must rise by an amount equal to the target rate of increase in the volume of housing plus the target of increase in house prices.

Thus both the aggregate rate of increase and the composition of Building Society advances will be fixed by the Government. How these advances are divided up among individual borrowers and areas and types of property may be left to the Societies themselves, although the Government could issue directives also in this regard — e.g., with respect to first-time buyers, development areas, urban renewal projects.

It is of course unlikely that Building Society deposits will increase at exactly the same rate as advances under this scheme of regulation. The Government must therefore be prepared to supplement, or siphon off, deposits. For example, if mandatory advances outstrip deposits, the Government must lend the Societies the difference, at the rate of interest paid to depositors. Similarly, if deposits outstrip the mandatory level of advances, the Societies must be obliged to lend the Government the difference, receiving the rate of interest paid by mortgage-borrowers. Incidentally, this entire scheme presupposes that the Government will keep the interest rate paid on mortgages sufficiently low so that the flow of mortgages is always, as it has been up to now in England, limited by quantitative rationing by the Societies, rather than by reluctance to borrow on the part of potential home-owners. This in itself will have consequences for the interest rate paid to depositors, and thus for the flow of deposits — although, much of the money lent to Societies is attracted by factors other than the gross return, and the whole system would be gravely destabilised if the "hot money" element were to predominate.

All this of course boils down to the Government of Scotland regulating the Building Societies in the same way that the U.K. Government has regulated the banking system, with directives on the amount and composition of lending, the freezing and unfreezing of special deposits, etc. Indeed, given the high priority which all modern Governments have attached to housing, it is quite incredible that Building Society lending should have been allowed to pursue a haphazard *laisser-faire* course. The scheme proposed here, or some variant of it, would permit Building Society lending to be an integral part of a centrally planned housing policy; if it is to succeed, however, it is essential that the Government should not slip into the easy folly of using centrally directed Building Society lending as a tool of short-term demand management.

Nationalisation?

It might be argued, given this degree of direction, and given too the inexorable march of the existing Societies towards at least a big-ten oligopoly, if not an outright monopoly, that we might just as well nationalise the lot, and run a State Building Society, or a Housing Bank. In fact, there are powerful arguments in Scotland for the new State to offer mortgage facilities — but not, I think, to monopolise them.

The existing large Societies demonstrate all the vices of bureaucracy; inflexible lending, arbitrary rules, burgeoning staffs and premises. If the State is to intervene, it should be to redress their failings, not augment them; and, whether directly or through the local authorities, supply an alternative source of funds to those borrowers, and for those properties and districts, which the Societies cannot or will not handle. Much of the problem could be solved once the Societies grow accustomed to social direction. If they are told that Scotland cannot accept rules based on English experience — no tenement flats opening on to the street, no properties without mains services, no lending in Joppa or Lewis or whatever—but must lend within the Scottish experience, preference, and need, no doubt they will. The alternative need scarcely be stated. The State might also intervene to curtail the appetites of the large Societies for the small, since it is the smaller ones which tend to display genuine local knowledge and sympathy.

Nevertheless, we must not lose sight of the fact that the argument in favour of expanding owner-occupation is pragmatic, not doctrinaire. If it diverts voluntary private savings and earnings into houses, it is likely to be more efficient, and effective, than any process whereby reluctant taxation is applied to building. If it prolongs the useful lives of dwellings, and maintains them at the rising level of common expectation, it is relatively cheap. And if it responds to the market demand of the consumer, it is likely to create more satisfying communities than the fiat from above. We have no right to say what people ought to want, or ought to be, if we give them no opportunity to establish their own wants, and their own satisfactions.

The Public Sector

Accordingly, there is no reason why we should not apply the same approach to the present public sector, or the present and future rented sector. There are no bad soldiers, only bad officers. Unfortunately, Scotland has suffered from the conviction that the people cannot be trusted, and that they must be told; and the officers have not been as good as they might.

This understanding can be seen struggling to be free in Robin Cook's excellent study of the housing problem in last year's "Red Paper";[1] unfortunately, since Mr Cook is imprisoned in the Labour Party, he had at all times to evade the doctrinal heresies of private ownership and consumer democracy. Recognising the problem, he could not admit the solutions, for to do so would be to abandon his party's claim to the divine right of management. Instead of embracing occupier democracy, whether by notional ownership or by co-operative management or market freedom, he had to fall back on the call for more professional housing management.

There is no doubt that professional housing managers do a better job than city architects or venal councillors; but how much more impressive if the ultimate consumers of the product are given sovereignty. Left to the consumer, we would never build another Pilton, another Whitfield, another Ferguslie; left to the consumer, we would not have torn down Tollcross, nor the city centres of Glasgow and Dundee. The consumer wants a better bathroom, and should have one too; but the consumer knows that life is more than bathrooms galore at the furthest reach of the city's bus routes.

The proof of this is now so familiar that only those who dare not see can still deny. What we must do is not waste time in political invective, or even breast-beating, but accept the situation. The new Scotland will inherit a grotesque portfolio of housing, much of which must necessarily be kept in use for a generation. It cannot be razed, much less forgotten; and so it must be reformed as best we can.

Tenants Co-Management

The first step is to make it plain to the tenants that they have the biggest say in their own environment. They must be offered the reality of purchase — and even the most obscurantist councillor must recognise the blessing it would be to all the other social services if the housing debt were shifted from the local authority on to the willing shoulders of the occupants. But if they do not want to purchase, either on principle or in their present premises, they must be given the reality of tenant consultation and management. From little things — the immediate right to keep pets, paint the door, change the letterbox — to large, like the right to inherit or transfer tenancy, the victims of our present system must be granted human rights.

The consumer's rights to consultation must be defined and guaranteed with some urgency. Whether or not the title to public-sector houses is transferred from local authorities and the S.S.H.A. (and the Coal Board and the Forestry Commission and a variety of other marginal landlords) to a single Government agency, tenents' co-management is essential. And if it is essential in already existing schemes, it is essential before another public-sector house is built. Instead of allowing burgh architects to build, and then expecting housing departments to inherit, we must bring in the putative occupants at the first stage of all. Nobody knows best what ought to be provided; nobody, that is, more than those whose lives and families will be shaped by that provision. If the people want gardened bungalows, or courtyard tenements, nothing in our experience of modern planning can argue that the people are wrong, and the planners right. The worst overcrowding in Scotland, an overcrowded nation, is to be found on modern council schemes; they were not designed with that in view — they were indeed designed to break up the huddled intimacy of the slums, and introduce the room-occupancy of fashionable theory. But average statistical families of 4.6 persons take in granny, son-in-law and cousin Jimmy, not only to shelter them in hard times, but because they genuinely want a closer-knit and supportive grouping. The family barricaded against the bailiffs in the single-end is a familiar story; but nobody fights to stay in a tower block miles from their work, their friends, their family and the shops.

As for the existing properties, it should be the immediate objective of a Scottish Government to ensure that every tenant be granted full participation in a localised co-management scheme. Localised should mean just that; it would be fatuous to accept the present delimitation, and assume that every tenant at Castlemilk or Craigmillar was part of a single management community. In fact, there is no lower limit for these groups — where a small burgh has a distinct scheme of barely 20 homes, that must be the participant community — but there is a common-sense upper limit. It may vary according to the type and density of dwellings in a scheme, but it should not perhaps exceed the size of a political ward — say 5,000 adults — and it might be better if the target were kept as low as 1,000 families. It would be part of that community's function to help decide the rate at which their area should grant individual or collective rights of purchase, as well as to take over questions of amenity. It is unquestionably desirable that we move to a broader social mix in our existing one-class schemes but this can be achieved by spontaneous local response more easily than by some form of external direction.

The present management bodies would obviously cede many of their responsibilities and their powers but they would still have a vital role to play. Theirs would be the job of reporting local needs and goals to the central Government so that the national targets could be best distributed across the land; theirs too would be the job of renewal and renovation, and of meeting the demand, almost ignored at present, for specialised housing for the elderly and disabled, for the single, and the transient. These tasks sit well together. There could be no better use for modernised city-centre properties than to cater for the mixed community which most benefits from easy access — the pensioners, the sick, the young working couples, the students. These people include those who are never likely to want, or be able, to purchase, and those who are beginning to save for a purchase to be made at some later stage. The destruction of city centres, and of the private-rented sector, in the pursuit of standardised two and three-apartment dwellings on vast new estates, has left them by the wayside. Once more, we need to create a mix in our communities and that mix should not merely be by class or income, but by age and interest as well. There is nothing more depressing than the scheme which begins as a monstrous suburban creche, all young mothers and their children while the fathers travel off to work, inexorably becoming a jungle of bored and restless teenagers, and ends as a ghetto for the old, bearing all the marks of declining incomes and long-frustrated hopes.

Conclusion

It will be the privilege of a Scottish Government then to create a situation in which the resources, human and material, of its people may be directed best to the improvement of Scotland's housing. In which the role of planning is to optimise productivity, not maximise it. But it will above all be our task to restore the consumer to the central role, whether that consumer wishes to be assisted to bear individual responsibility, or requires instead to enjoy equal rights of citizenship whilst renting; both forms are equally respectable, although "private ownership" undoubtedly offers greater advantages to society as a whole, and both should enjoy equal status and equal rights. Not to punish, nor reward, but to serve.

1   Robin Cook, "Scotland's Housing", *The Red Paper on Scotland,* edited by Gordon Brown, Edinburgh, 1975, pp 334-351.

ENVIRONMENTAL POLICY IN AN INDEPENDENT SCOTLAND

David Purves

Man has no existence without his environment and the environment of any people sets limits to their welfare, their happiness and their quality of life. The environment is neither indestructable nor infinitely renewable; its protection is therefore fundamental to human existence.

It is now generally recognised that mankind faces an environmental crisis. The last decade has seen the foundation of the Club of Rome, the publication of a large body of "doomsday" literature (notably *A Blueprint for Survival,* 1971) and the establishment of environmental protection agencies in many countries.[1]

The root cause of this crisis is that European man has made no attempt to live in harmony with the environment and has consistently adopted an exploitative attitude towards it. Stable populations that are related to the potential for food production within the geographic space that is occupied have not been established. Implicit in this behaviour is the assumption that "progress" has meaning and can be measured in terms of economic growth, industrial expansion and population increase. My own view is that the sooner we dispense with such false notions of "progress" and turn to the goal of dynamic harmony the better.

Evolutionary Psychology

While it is not possible to do much more than speculate about the reasons why European man has acquired what can only be described as a set of cancerous psychological attitudes, the explanation is surely to be found in the harsh conditions in which our ancestors evolved. Evolutionary situations such as the succession of Ice Ages, in which the survival of whole tribal populations is at risk every winter, are peculiarly suited to the development of ruthless attitudes such as, "We must leave no stone unturned" and "Of what use are animals (and other humans)?" Our obsession with quantification (no doubt largely a device for estimating grain crops in the first instance) and technology is probably another consequence of our stringent evolutionary background.

The Scottish anthropologist, Sir Arthur Keith, has dealt at some length in his writings with the evolutionary basis of man's psychology but whatever the original causes of European man's distinctive attributes, it is now clear that we are saddled with them. We will have to make do with a mixed bag of instinctual feelings, such as, hostility towards members of out-groups, amity towards indentifiable members of in-groups, an obsession with quantification and a disposition to organise our activities into what we can persuade ourselves are purposeful projects (a kind of pseudo-hunt).

Since we now find that the social structure we have evolved can no longer accommodate these traits in our nature, we are obliged to seek an alternative structure in which the constructive and co-operative elements in our nature will receive encouragement. Our aggressive tendencies must be channelled into inter-community competitive activities like sport, for example. The only global social pattern that meets these requirements is a decentralised society based on small, independent, internally decentralised and largely self-sufficient nations.

In considering what might be suitable policies for an independent Scotland, we are, necessarily, concerned with objectives which are valid for the world as a whole. We must therefore seek a Scotland which could provide a model for an international society based on such communities.

Shrinking Resources

The principle cause of the environmental crisis is overpopulation exacerbated by an economic system which relies on rapidly and permanently increasing consumption of manufactured goods per capita. Since the economic system operates within the context of an advanced technology, in both its capitalist and communist variant, the environmental impact associated with constantly increasing productivity and an exploding population is now catastrophic. We face the prospect of exhaustion of fossil fuels and irreplaceable mineral resources and widespread environmental pollution from radio-active and chemical wastes.

According to *A Blueprint for Survival,* mankind is rapidly using up global reserves of metal ores. At present rates of consumption all known reserves of silver, gold, lead, tin and zinc will be exhausted before the year 2000. The indispensable element, copper, will run out a few years later and by the year 2150 the only metals with known reserves will be iron and chromium. The situation appears even more serious if we assume an exponential increase in metal consumption, such as has occured since 1960, for on this basis, all known metal reserves would be exhausted within 50 years, with the exception of iron and chromium. Although the latter scenario is the most pessimistic possible, and takes no account of the possible discovery of new ore reserves, the overall picture is alarming whatever figures we choose as a basis of calculating the length of time metal reserves might last.

The urgent need to conserve non-renewable supplies of metals reinforces the need to prevent pollution problems arising from their dispersion into the environment. These two problems are complementary.

The general situation is made much more serious than it might be by the present economic thinking and its limited horizons. The conventional wisdom tends to be based on the assumption that the Earth's resources are inexhaustible and can therefore be treated as income. In addition human progress is identified with never-ending economic growth, industrial expansion which is dependent on overseas markets and constantly rising consumption of material goods per head of population. With the possible exception of the Scottish National Party, all political parties in the United Kingdom are committed to this materialistic view of social progress, even though it is becoming increasingly obvious that this course cannot be sustained indefinitely and must eventually lead, if not checked, to socio-economic collapse.

The Quality of Life

The S.N.P. is exceptional in the emphasis it has placed on the quality of life and on its long-standing recognition of the desirability of national self-sufficiency. It has also emphasised that Scotland's future prosperity depends on avoiding overpopulation through over-industrialisation or from any other reason. These beliefs are associated witht the belief in the value of small communities with which individuals can identify themselves and in the principle of decentralisation of government.

The general trend in the S.N.P. is towards an environmentalist position, though it would be wrong to suggest that the party had already arrived at such a position. There are people in the S.N.P. who still regard industrial expansion and unrestricted movement of labour across national boundaries to suit the interests of capital, as good things in themselves and who would be quite happy to see Scotland burdened with a population of 10 million to support.

In formulating policy for an independent Scotland, it will have to be recognised that the environmental crisis is global in scope and that the present pattern of international trade which is based on the assumption that it will always be possible to transport goods from any part of the world to wherever there is a local demand has created a situation where no nation can achieve more than partial self-sufficiency in food, energy and essential raw materials. In an inter-dependent world there are limits to independence for all nations and an economic policy based on international co-operation is essential if we are to reduce the tensions engendered by the great disparities in national resources which exist.

The wealth of a nation is the quality of life it can permanently support and this must be measured in terms of its renewable resources, such as agriculture, forestry, fisheries and hydro-power in relation to its total population. The key to any environmental policy is therefore a population policy based on the belief that the community which is Scotland should live in harmony with the environment. This must mean a policy of conserving its heritage of natural resources (of which the oil in North Sea is an important part) for the benefit of future generations.[2]

Population Policy

The present population of Scotland is around five million. Although it is badly distributed as a result of the industrial revolution in the central belt and the Highland clearances, the population is in reasonable balance with the size and resources of the country. It is both socially and economically desirable that it should not be substantially increased.

In the long term when Scotland's non-renewable resources have been exhausted, and we are obliged to fall back on agriculture, forestry, fisheries and hydro-power as our principle means of economic support, it may well be that even a population of five million will become excessive. In the interim, the importance of recycling non-renewable raw materials, such as metals and fertiliser nutrient, and of providing the infra-structure necessary for an economy based on renewable resources, cannot be over-estimated.

The foundation of any comprehensive environmental policy is population balance. Extra mouths put an additional strain on the nation's resources and few desirable objectives can be attained without an assurance of adequate living space. It is evident that this cannot be reconciled with the expansionist policy at present pursued by the European Economic Community and made worse by the development of a rootless itinerant labour force across Europe.

There are only two acceptable ways in which a Scottish government could control the size of the population: it could encourage family planning through education and the provision of effective birth control facilities and it can regulate immigration, mainly by employing a system of work permits.

A Scottish Ministry of the Environment

The activities of any government department or ministry can have environmental implications. Fields of particular relevance in this respect include: population, industry, resource management, transport, waste disposal, recycling, reclamation, conservation, recreation, tourism, amenity, urban and rural planning, land use, agriculture and land tenure. Clearly no single ministry could be responsible for government functions in all these areas and if a Ministry of the Environment was established it would have to possess widespread co-ordinating and advisory roles in addition to a specific area of responsibility.

Although such a ministry would be generally responsible for the quality of life in Scotland, the successful implementation of an environmental policy would depend on the acceptance and understanding by all government departments of the efficacy of the policy. A Scottish Ministry of the Environment, in contrast to the Westminster model, would have to oppose industrial interests when these are in conflict with the public interest.

The functions of economic development in an independent Scotland should be to provide full employment, eliminate poverty, social deprivation and urban squalor and to raise the standard of living to a level acceptable in a civilised Western society. Such is the level of social deprivation in Scotland — 97.5% of the areas of worst social deprivation are in Scotland according to the Department of the Environment — that a relatively high economic-growth rate will be necessary for some years after independence. This must be achieved with a stable population and indigenous resources. The objective will be to sustain this higher standard of living for the whole population.

In planning economic policy, it will be necessary to make a distinction between renewable resources and Scotland's heritage of irreplaceable resources, such as coal and off-shore oil. An obvious policy for Scotland would be to develop the former and conserve the latter in recognition that fossil fuel is an asset whose value to the Scottish people, and the world as a whole, will increase the more slowly it is extracted. Priority would therefore be given to the development of renewable resources of energy over fossil or nuclear fuels. So long as Scotland has control of adequate alternative energy sources it cannot be regarded as being in the national interest to generate power from nuclear fission reactors producing plutonium or other radio-active wastes which present problems of safe disposal.

Environmental Protection Agency

Environmental pollution either from radio-active or chemical wastes is a serious side-effect of the environmental crisis. Much of this pollution is highly persistent. Radio-active wastes may remain a hazard for thousands of years. Toxic metals and toxic organic compounds applied to the land as pesticides may remain in a contaminated soil for long periods, where they may enter biological food chains.

The public must be protected against health hazards arising from

G

environmental pollution and damage to amenity caused by industrial development and public works. This need has been recognised in the United States and in a number of other countries by the establishment of Environmental Protection Agencies. It is necessary that such agencies should be quasi-judicial bodies independent of direct political control so that they can act in the public interest without fear or favour. A Scottish Environmental Protection Agency, with teeth, is essential and this body would have the vitally important role of protecting the quality of life of the people.

The agency would have access to industrial sites, it would be empowered to require private and public bodies with major planning projects to justify any environmental impact arising from their projects and its findings in relation to any project would be made public. A primary consideration in assessing environmental impact would be the extent to which developments encroached on land capable of agricultural use. The agency would be charged to act in the interests of the general public and empowered to prohibit activities contravening codes of practice.

It is therefore envisaged that the quality of life in an independent Scotland would be secured by two bodies: a Ministry of the Environment with a conservationist orientation, implementing genuine environmental policies and an Environmental Protection Agency, protected from sectional interests by law and having a separate "watchdog" function.

1   D. Meadows *et al. The Limits to Growth,* London, 1972; *A Blueprint for Survival,* London, 1971; Gordon Rattray Taylor, *The Doomsday Book,* London, 1970.
2   Malcolm Slesser, *Scotland and Energy,* Fletcher Paper No. 3, Dundee, 1976.

92

INDUSTRIAL RELATIONS

Peter Craigie

As we stand within sight of the creation of an independent state in Scotland our generation is facing one of the most exciting prospects ever to confront our nation. As our political and economic life emerges from the long chrysalis stage of our union with England we must however recognise that the new state will face many difficulties. The road to full realisation of our national potential will be difficult and at times dangerous. It seems to me therefore of the greatest importance that the Scottish National Party recognises the more predictable dangers and realises that independence in itself is not enough. We must face up to the enormous task of creating a new society in Scotland based on greater social justice in every aspect of our national life.

The aspect of social justice I consider in this paper is Industrial Relations and I do this for two principal reasons. First, because in the period immediately following independence it is vital that the new Scottish government can demonstrate to the public at home and abroad that our industrial peace and stability is unquestioned and that it can work realistically with the labour movement. Second, because in our longer term pursuit of a more just and humane society it is necessary to consider the kind of industrial relations we seek. The life of people at work is an important strand in the total social tapestry and it is difficult to see how a modern, socially just society can be constructed around an industrial environment in which conflict is a destructive factor.

Let me make it clear that in this paper I take a broad view of the term industrial relations, using it in its widest sense to mean not only the collective relations between employers and trade unions but also the whole range of formal and informal relationships between individuals and organisations in industry and the effect on them of the social, political and economic environment.

Work and Industrial Relations

It is often said that management gets the industrial relations it deserves. Equally a society creates its own industrial relations, which reflect the attitudes and values of the society in which they exist. In dealing with the question of the kind of industrial relations we wish in an independent Scotland we are therefore forced to ask ourselves fundamental questions about the kind of society we seek and the values we wish it to retain or develop. These questions include something as apparently simple as our view of work. Is work a necessary evil, as is implied in the way in which the human element is eliminated whenever possible from large scale capital-intensive industries? Or is work rather an important human activity, capable of satisfying the essentially human needs of creativity and self-fulfilment and the need to share with others in a common task? What kind of society do we create if we ask our people to commit a major part of their lives to work which has been deliberately and systematically dehumanised and degraded into meaningless, trivial and boring repetition?

These considerations raise an important point. In planning our new society, the industrial relations aspects must be considered at the very earliest stage. We must, as it were, design in good industrial relations at the drawing board stage. We must scrutinise the nature and scale of our economic development, rather than trust to luck and our native wit or good nature to see us out of unanticipated but inevitable difficulties which are a result of the way we organise work.

As a party, we have in the past expressed our expectation that a new hope and spirit will develop within the Scottish workforce following the achievement of independence and that the release of latent energy and initiative which will follow will prove to be the greatest asset an independent Scottish government will inherit. While in no way denying this possibility, at least as a short term benefit, I would prefer us to take a more realistic view of the situation and to plan carefully how we intend to improve our industrial relations environment. I do not believe that this will be achieved merely by change in the control of enterprise from private to public ownership nor do I believe we should seek an industrial relations environment which is totally free from conflict.

What then would represent an improved industrial relations environment? From an economic point of view good industrial relations are simple. From this limited viewpoint, what we require is a system which permits sensible and, if necessary, rapid adjustments to the size of the labour force; flexible training arrangements and working practices which can be adapted to meet change in total demand or technology; suitable payment structures under the control of management which encourage increased productivity without excessive overtime and without creating wage drift.

We need flexibility in the pattern of working hours and, of course, we must avoid the disruptive effects of official, and more importantly, unofficial stoppages of work. All of this is a highly rational approach. Indeed the thinking implicit in this approach has been entitled "enterprise rationality".[1] It has also been called the logic of getting maximum results at minimum costs and even "the dictatorship of the balance sheet".[2] As enterprises increase in size of course, this rational approach leads to greater division and specialization of labour, and emphasizes the need for more administration and organisational discipline. It is therefore in the large scale organisation that the full potential for conflict in industry appears.

The history of large scale mass production enterprises such as the car industry or the steel industry, to take examples from public ownership, presents a sorry picture. In such organisations enterprise rationality backed by organisational discipline in pursuit of efficiency meets another element in the industrial relations system, "human non-rationality", the term which describes the reactions of the order-takers to the order-givers in a situation in which the order-taker is basically concerned to limit or modify the effect of organisational discipline so as to make it more tolerable to his objectives. These are usually concerned less with efficiency and more with issues such as personal and job security, status or group solidarity. The result, often inexplicable to the observer, is an ongoing conflict of varying levels of intensity. What tends to exacerbate this conflict of objectives is the fact that the groups who pursue these conflicting objectives within the workplace tend to be drawn from different social classes.

It would be naive to pretend that social differences do not exist between managers and workers. Outside of the workplace the two groups are likely to live in physically different surroundings and have different life-styles. Membership of different socio-economic groups inevitably affects attitudes and behaviour.

Role of Conflict

The classical Marxist view of this conflict is that it is an inevitable and desirable process leading to the collapse of the capitalist system. Managers see it as an aberration from common sense and logic. Trade unions tend to alternate between condemnation of the conflict (where the union is pursuing its co-operative function with management aimed at increasing the efficiency of the organisation and its ability to pay wages) and support of the conflict (when the union feels the need to display militancy to ensure its own group solidarity). Practical industrial relations is therefore the management of this conflict. In other words, our industrial relations system must allow us to use conflict constructively by channelling and institutionalising it, rather than by ignoring it or hoping to eliminate it.

The conflict I have described between enterprise rationality and human non-rationality is by definition essentially a human conflict, which exists whenever the objectives of an enterprise conflict with the objectives of the individuals in it. In an independent Scotland, what should our attitude to this conflict be? I suggest that we must begin by accepting as reality that some conflict in industry and class conflict in our society is inevitable which will not be eliminated simply by new systems of representation, improved negotiating procedures or by changes in the ownership of the enterprise. We must recognise that class conflicts exist in Scotland and that they will continue to exist for some time, perhaps for a long time, after independence. They will not fade away in a new golden age of brotherhood, fellowship and national commitment, however desirable that might be.

I am not, of course, suggesting that we accept the *status quo*. The Scottish National Party is essentially a pragmatic party, that is to say a non-ideological party. The pragmatic approach is well described as that which views a difficulty as something to be worked on rather than as something to be hated. As William James says, "A pragmatist turns away from fixed principles, closed systems and pretended absolutes and origins. He turns towards concreteness and adequacy, towards facts, towards action".[3]

What I suggest is that our method of dealing with class and industrial conflict must be to actively present an alternative to the ideological positions taken by socialist and capitalist theorists. We must develop and publicise our pragmatic non-ideological view of society. I believe that this should be based on the *fact* that class conflict exists and that in every aspect of our social and economic policies we strive for two basic elements. First, that we eliminate the exploitation of one class by another and, second, that we ensure that the wealth of our society is distributed on an equitable basis such that each person in society is able to enjoy a decent standard of living. In this way the inevitable conflict can be robbed of its most destructive elements.

Democratic Management

The practical consequence of this view is that we must launch a multiple attack on the structure of our existing industrial society. Different forms of ownership must be experimented with, profit sharing must be mandatory. Employee participation in decision-making must be increased by representation at board level and by the development of elected works councils. Policy decisions must be scrutinised by supervisory boards containing representatives of the social interest as well as work's directors.

In this context it is worth noting that the Scottish National Party's proposals for a two-tier board structure, with the supervisory board composed equally of representatives for the social interest, employees and shareholders, is broadly in line with the views expressed in the European Parliament last year when the draft of the European Common Statute was debated. In addition, the draft Fifth Directive of the E.E.C. and its successor, the E.E.C. Green Paper published in November 1975 are both committed to the concept of two-tier boards.

The control of the executives by a "watch-dog" board which includes representatives of the employees, although greeted with a chorus of alarm in conservative circles, has a highly respectable pedigree going back as far as the Liberal Yellow Book and their proposals of 1928.[4] There is of course also a substantial body of experience derived from German and Dutch industry. One can even see parallels in the bastion of capitalism, the United States, where the practise has developed for the executive group of President and Vice-Presidents to be supervised by the full board, who are expected to take a wider view of corporate responsibility to the employees and the community.

It is of course one thing to alter the formal legal and representative structure of industry and quite another to change the way people feel and behave on the shop floor. As well as the legalistic structural approach to change, it is therefore imperative that new and more democratic patterns of management are introduced to industry at all levels. The key to this seems to be in extensive training, using established behavioural science techniques, so that managers and trade union representatives learn how to use conflict creatively rather than destructively. A considerable amount of knowledge already exists in this field and companies should be encouraged to apply it, possibly stimulated by the payment of direct grants from government. It is important however that human relations and communication techniques are used, not to smooth over, but to bring to the surface the issues that divide and create conflict so that they can be confronted realistically, and dealt with by the parties concerned.

Beyond the questions of techniques there is also an important question of philosophy which must be considered. We must face the problem of scale in our industrial society. It is clear that organisational patterns need to be developed to allow us to deal with the problems of communication, so that individuals can feel that they play a meaningful part in the system. This has been recognised in countries like Sweden and Italy where it is becoming accepted that the de-skilled, mass-production approach to the car industry, although in theory the most economic, contains serious hidden human problems. Boring and repetitive work, especially if it is demanded of skilled and intelligent craftsmen, creates an atmosphere in which grievances and strikes flourish. Less dramatic but equally costly is a high rate of absenteeism. High wage rates have done little to overcome the natural human distaste for this type of work and indeed, as in the Swedish experience, merely allows people to afford to stay away from work. With expensive capital equipment, this has forced companies like Volvo and Fiat to look again at the classic theories of flow-line production and work simplification and to revert to small work groups with greater autonomy, building a more complete product.

The work re-structuring in Volvo has been well documented but there is another, lesser-known example from Sweden which may be equally relevant to our situation. Holmens Bruk[5], a large pulp and paper manufacturer has used a bold and imaginative approach to building a new pulp mill at Braviken, where they will employ about 320 people. Through a series of committees they have involved their employees fully in the detailed design and planning of the mill, literally from the drawing board stage, including the delicate business of phasing the closure of an older mill and the transfer of its work load. There has been an ongoing employee involvement not only in matters such as safety and working conditions but also in financial and production target setting, which in this country are rarely conceded by management to be matters legitimately the concern of the employees. It seems to me that there is much we can learn from this model, particularly the involvement of the "doers" in the planning process. Too often in this country we separate the "planners" and the "doers" into distinct groups (with inherent status implications) and then wait for the "inevitable" complaints from the workforce who have to live with the results.

People Matter

However desperately we need to create employment we must examine carefully proposed new developments to ensure that the work and the total working environment created fulfil certain basic criteria. In the words of Dr. Schumacher "They must give our people the chance to develop and utilise their faculties". He goes on to say, "What is the meaning of democracy, freedom, human dignity, standard of living, self-realisation, fulfilment — is it a matter of goods or of people? Of course it is a matter of people. But people can be themselves only in small comprehensible groups, therefore we must learn to think in terms of articulated structures that can cope with a multiplicity of small scale units. If economic thinking cannot grasp this it is useless."[6]

I have tried to describe the kind of approach by which I believe we can create in Scotland a stable industrial society, capable of generating and fairly distributing sufficient material wealth to raise the vast bulk of our people from the disgraceful social conditions in which they have been left by 250 years of political impotence. As we achieve this however I hope we will not lose sight of the need to create for our people not only material well-being, desirable though that is, but also a society in which work is not simply a means to buy possessions or to achieve leisure but is a worthwhile and necessary part of life. Then we will have created a Scotland worthy of independence and an example to the rest of the world.

1   Ben Seligman, *Main Currents in Modern Economics,* London 1962.
2   Cael Landauer, *European Socialism,* London 1959, Volume 2.
3   William James, *Pragmatism — a new name for old ways of thinking,* New York 1907.
4   Liberal Party, *Britain's Industrial Future: Report of the Liberal Enquiry,* 1928.
5   Institute of Personnel Management, "Participation from the Shop Floor Up", *Journal of the Institute of Personnel Management,* Volume 8, No. 2.
6   E. F. Schumacher, *Small is Beautiful: a study of economics as if people mattered,* London 1973.

SOCIALISM OR NATIONALISM?

Owen Dudley Edwards

All of the Red Paper's[1] contributors believed themselves to be socialists, and the bulk of them were, in some sense of the term, nationalists; all of our contributors believe themselves to be nationalists, and the bulk of them are, in some sense of the term, socialists. So we would hold that a Scottish socialism which fails to come to terms with nationalism is in some way defective, and so is a Scottish nationalism which fails to address itself to the challenge of socialism. A socialist without a head is as monstrous as a nationalist without a heart.

In all of this, we are the victims of the prostitution of terminology. "Nationalist" is a dirty word to many socialists who evoke visions of the late unlamented Hitler and the lamented unlate I.R.A. "Socialist" is a dirty word to many nationalists who with equal lack of justification tie it to the computer-type bureaucracy of a soulless dictatorial metropolis. At least there is a common ground in seeing the unfairness with which each term is treated.

There remains for each ideology the challenge of their opponents. Invincible ignorance will prove as hardy a perennial in response to both socialism and nationalism as it has proved against other religious faiths. And however great our detestation of the doctrinal abominations called Unionism or capitalism we both have the same thankless duty of hating the sin and loving the sinner.

If we deny that Hitler was a true nationalist or Stalin a true socialist we must also deny ourselves the use of their characteristic answers, those of creating "national enemies" or "class enemies". If we are strong enough against false doctrine, we can prevail against false votaries. Their bases of power we must destroy; they themselves we must always seek to convert. The most repulsively Unionist capitalist is in doctrinal terms our enemy; but when we declare him an "unperson" we diminish our own title to humanity thereby.

A very great Scottish socialist and nationalist, James Connolly, wrote, "Organise for a full, free and happy life, FOR ALL OR FOR NONE." This in my view has to be the principle which should animate both movements, in every respect.

It is of course natural that we deal in personal terms. To deal in personalities is not only natural for human beings, it also gets a debate into concrete terms where the abstract either leads to confusion or else to an ultimate departure from human realities. But between the convenience of rhetoric and the capitulation to hatred there must lie an impassable barrier. If our faiths have any justification, it must be that they are causes of love always and of hatred never. The frightful crimes that have been committed throughout history in the name of socialism and in the name of nationalism are a grim reminder of what happens when that barrier is transcended.

There is no faith so noble that it cannot be perverted; there is no person so secure that he cannot fall. And if we can be acquitted of the venality of

Hitler and Stalin, are we immune from the fearful incorruptibility of Robespierre?

Social Democracy?

To return to the word-problem, it is significant how comparable is the vulnerability it gives to both socialists and nationalists. George Orwell could have written the script: "Devolution — good; separatism — bad. Social democracy — good; socialism — bad." These are the sheep's slogans, and the more fashionable they become, the more they should remind us that their acceptance is an abandonment of the thinking process.

I suppose I could be charged with some sheepism myself, or sheepism in reverse, with my lack of enthusiasm for the term "social democracy". It is true that my dislike of it largely derives from the company it has kept. If social democracy means democratic socialism, I heartily subscribe to it: I would advocate no other kind of socialism. The trouble is that many people who have recently termed themselves "social democrats" seem much more conspicuous for their hostility to socialism than for any support for its cause.

We have in the S.N.P. many self-styled "social democrats", not one of whom I would link with this doubtful company. But two points need to be made to them. The first is that most of them appear to be socialists in any case, so why not rejoice in the name? Secondly, it is much less likely that we in Scotland will be captured by Hitlers or Stalins than we might be subverted by the soft infection of United States political and economic influence.

The bad odour which clings around the words "socialism" and "nationalism" is a form of insurance; in the Scottish context, the U.S. Government has made it abundantly clear that it is no friend to either, and if I am worried by the Hitlers and Stalins that lie in embryo in every human being, I have less reason to worry that a non-violent party like the S.N.P. could be infiltrated by the I.R.A. or that the Kremlin might polish up its accent to participate in the singing of "Scots Wha Hae".

We are all prone to become patsies for less-scrupulous people; but social democrats have throughout history shown a propensity for being used by people of an unusual adeptness in concealing their lack of scruple. A firmness in identifying ourselves at the outset does much to keep diplomacy out of the shadows. And, as was preached though not practised by Woodrow Wilson, good diplomacy thrives in the light.

The S.L.P.

The relationship of these present essays to the Red Paper involves a personal point for me. I was one of the two S.N.P. writers who contributed to it; and the other one, Mr Bob Tait, has left the S.N.P. and entered the Scottish Labour Party.[2] I am regretful that a fine editor of an excellent and tragically defunct periodical, *Scottish International*, should have departed our ranks. On rereading his essay in the Red Paper I am inclined to feel that its arguments tell strongly against his present stance, but it is wise to remember that Mr Tait is a poet, and poets are not subject to the normal rules of logic.

But Mr Tait's departure from S.N.P. ranks leaves me, as the survivor, in a curious situation. It is as though a fellow Roman Catholic had contributed with me to a multi-author ecumenical work and had then left the Church. I wish to leave neither Church nor party. Yet I am conscious of my fellow contributor's devotion to ideologies I also hold; I feel a personal sense of bereavement; I fear for the injury which his defection may do to the causes in which we both believe.

In fine, I can see the possibility of a curious agreement between certain elements in S.N.P. and S.L.P. to the effect that socialists who are nationalists. belong in the S.L.P. I do not believe that this view is beneficial for the cause of socialism or for the cause of nationalism. I am convinced that the mass of the S.N.P., if they think about it, will indignantly repudiate such a doctrine; I trust that those in the S.L.P. who are more socialist than political will see the danger it poses for the future of their own creed. It is a problem which may be of more consequence in the future than in the present.

At the time of writing, the S.L.P. has yet to show that it is more than a fan club for Mr Jim Sillars; or a think-piece by Mr Neal Ascherson; or a tutorial by Mr Tom Nairn; or a potential resting-place for Mr Jimmy Reid; or a means of fraternal distinction for Mr Andrew Brown; or an area for folklore research for Mr Hamish Henderson; or a source of poetic inspiration to Mr Bob Tait. They are all charming people and as I have always found Hampstead one of the most agreeable places in London, now that the railway fares have become so monstrous, why should we not have a little Hampstead of our own?

Hampstead is a nice place to visit, but I wouldn't like to live there. The same is true of the S.L.P. if it somehow survives the storm-clouds rolling over its infant head to become a major party in Scotland. For all of its impressive literary membership, it demands our charity at this juncture. Its personnel on the firing-line are fighting for many things in which the S.N.P. believes, and Mr Sillars in particular is being subjected to every aspect of the brutish and cruel weaponry at the disposal of the British Labour party; as he has pointedly remarked, Mr John Stonehouse received a markedly more tender treatment from that party than he did. Of course, Mr Stonehouse was neither a nationalist nor a socialist, and Mr Sillars is showing dangerous signs of being both. But what guarantee has Mr Sillars that his party, hewn from the same materials as its unnatural parent, will not equal its achievement by producing its own Stonehouses or its own Harold Wilsons?

Socialists who argue that the S.N.P. is unpalatable because it contains many members who say they are not socialists should ask themselves how well socialism has fared at the hands of parties the majority of whose members say they are socialists? I heartily welcome anything the S.L.P. can do to advance the cause of socialism and nationalism in Scotland. But it is worth remembering that the S.L.P., by its own existence, is an admission that the Labour Party in Scotland has failed, and we have no insurance against a repeat performance. It is idle to point out that Mr Jim Sillars is a high-principled man; the British Labour Party was built up on the highest of principles. As for the nice intellectuals around him, they make my blood run cold. The Labour Party machinery for most of its existence has been taking nice intellectuals for a ride; now they have revolted, but their only answer is to build another Labour Party.

Socialism and the S.N.P.

I want to argue, therefore, that it is not the S.L.P. (useful and constructive though many of its contributions may prove to be) but the S.N.P.

which offers the real promise of socialism in Scotland. There are many members of the S.N.P. who call themselves socialists in public; there are more who call themselves socialists in private; there are many so-called social democrats who seem possessed of an acceptable down payment on intellectual commitment to socialism; and there are many members who do not call themselves socialists but who hold more socialist ideas than many professed votaries of the faith.

There appears to be a major confusion in socialism between those who are socialists and those who talk in class terms. The latter is very easy; it throws up a defensive apparatus behind which a great deal can shelter. Class is in fact one of the easiest rhetorics to exploit. Orwell can be cited eloquently on that point. The effects are inimical to socialism in a number of ways. There will be the workers who are out for larger and larger slices of the capitalist cake, which accounts for the fate of the great bulk of the labour leadership in the U.S.A. and these islands. There will be the fascinated enquiry of devout Marxists into the ailments, contradictions, conspiracies and power of capitalism which, again notably in the U.S.A. and Britain, has so often ended in a naked worship of capitalism, perhaps buttressed by an alleged formal commitment to socialist labels, perhaps not. There is the theoretical Marxist who vigorously employs the language of class struggle to maintain a rigid conservatism in practice. There is, above all, the chance for the opportunist, who learns the parrot-cries quickly and thus wins the support of the sheep.

It is possible to see an easy equation between this problem and that of a narrow nationalism which is primarily negative and (in Scotland's case) Anglophobe.

The answer to both is that we want a positive nationalism and a positive socialism which cannot exist independently of one another.

The Land Question

The Red Paper on Scotland has the advantage of giving us a most positive perspective. It is nevertheless capable of both wasting our time and of sending us running up a defensive cul-de-sac. Indeed, to date, S.N.P. responses to it have been generous in private but often depressingly pedantic in public.

A cause as great as that of the S.N.P. cannot permit itself to be robbed of the virtue of self-criticism. Nor will it be served if it will only accept criticism swaddled in flattery. Its natural future converts may justly be expected to say many rude words as they make their pilgrimage. We have to be ready to take lessons from any useful source, including those far more intrinsically hostile to us than most of the contributors to the Red Paper.

There are, of course, certain points of total non-relationship. We need not concern ourselves with formal opposition such as that of Mr Jim Sillars, whose views on the land question seem akin to our own in everything but name, plus the fact that we are committed to more socialist policies on the matter than he is.[3] He is wise to relate what is desirable to what is possible — certain other very inspiring articles in Red Paper are in danger of assisting the *status quo* by enunciating an agenda so far beyond the bounds of achievement by forces within our control that they virtually invite their readers to feel socialist and do nothing.

Millenialism is inspirational, science fiction is fun and total inflexibility of principle induces highly gratifying sensations of personal virtue. Meanwhile the practicality we have scorned is left to our eminently resourceful enemies. This is also a danger for nationalism. Scottish nationalism is in a highly dynamic state at present. But its most fervent supporters, intoxicated by their general principles and unexpected success, can find themselves losing vital ground by failure to scrutinise seemingly petty but critical details on which the "practical" men can render total victory impossible.

Mr Sillars is more prone to the other pitfall, as indeed are most members of his former party. His sense of what is practical and feasible leads him here to ask for far less than what he should. He asserts the ideal of public ownership but seems to create a cleavage between it and "current political and economic realities".

The S.N.P., turning to the traditions of Henry George (on whose influence in Scotland Dr James Young has very helpful material in his essay),[4] relates land ownership to land use; and thereby places itself on a footing at once more practical and more radical than that occupied by Mr Sillars. Indeed, for all of the near-century between ourselves and George's great book, *Progress and Poverty*,[5] John McEwen's statistics on highland landlordism are a revelation on what relatively little change in the distribution of agrarian wealth and its resultant power Scotland has seen in the interim.[6]

Mr Sillars doubtless regards himself to the left of Mr Douglas Henderson; but Mr Henderson has eloquently asserted in the House of Commons our commitment to the principle that the land of Scotland is for those who work it as opposed to those who would maintain it as their pleasure-grounds or basis for profiteering. Indeed, as Henry George firmly asserted, the principle of keeping the land in the hands of those who work it themselves derives from biblical assertion. With all respect to Mr Sillars, the unnatural seizure of the land by profiteers simply cannot be permitted to continue. The future of Scotland must turn on our policy of testing land use, and those who fail to justify their possession of the land on a basis of personal production will simply lose it. This is not confiscation; it is the operation of implicit penalty clauses in a contract.

The point is one which eloquently points up the interrelationship of nationalism and socialism. If we believe in Scotland as a nation, we must insist that its resources cannot be squandered to the injury of the country and the community in the interests of a selfish few. That principle must be applied to natural resources of all kinds, including oil. Meanwhile, as Mr Henderson has put it, if Scottish nationalism means anything at all, it means the end of the grouse moors. Nor is this a long-term ideal. In the present combination of dramatic constitutional change and general economic crisis, the time is now.

The Left and the S.N.P.

In certain other respects we will have differences with contributors to the Red Paper of a kind which not only look like being irreconcilable, but which ought to be. It does not get away from the fact that our ideological opponents, whether Right or Left, have lessons to teach us even if these are normally negative lessons. But when Mr Ray Burnett tells me that "the S.N.P. is no haven for a socialist" I am in agreement with him, given what I know to be his definition of socialism.[7] I applaud his devotion and idealism, and his readiness to subject himself to severe privations in the furtherance of his beliefs. But he supports a socialism which calls for action in Ireland of a kind certain to result in the deaths of many people. To me, a socialism which requires corpses is no socialism at all. So long as Mr Burnett, or anyone else, finds violence necessary or even acceptable in the furtherance of socialism, there will be no place for them in the S.N.P.

It is otherwise with points of personal disagreement. It is irritating, though doubtless ultimately for the good of our souls, for Mr Stephen Maxwell and for me to find ourselves taken to task by Mr Tom Nairn for nationalist mythologising. But if an occasional unkind and — we would argue — inaccurate footnote is going to advance Mr Nairn's excellent and constructive arguments, we will receive his pitchfork with as much serenity as the process can permit.[8] For Mr Nairn has produced over the years a series of papers deserving of the most thoughtful consideration by every Scottish nationalist and socialist. They have aroused much annoyance; and from nowhere have they received such severe reappraisal in succession as from Mr Nairn himself.

The progress of this brilliant and austere critic of Scottish nationalism from apparent hostility to eloquent and hortatory participation is in itself an unanswerable lesson to the critics of what is happening in Scotland. Many recent converts have been compared, with an originality diminished by repetition, to St Paul on the road to Damascus; Mr Nairn has offered us a spectacle awesome enough to rival Jacob's wrestling with his angel.

The S.N.P. is currently so overwhelmingly successful, and has to date by its performance done such dreadful execution on its critics, that it must be tempted to ignore many voices of warning. Mr Nairn's voice, for one, is not to be ignored. The bibliography of his critiques of Scottish nationalism technically commences with an article in 1967 entitled "Festival of the Dead".[9] It gave great offence at the time; and it is occasionally cited since then as an unanswerable case against so much that is false and culturally destructive in the Edinburgh Festival and in Scotland. "Society is language; Scotland is silence" was one of its lines. It is not unanswerable; Mr Nairn continues to answer it.

Indeed the very existence of this sort of assault reminds one of James Joyce's insistence on Dublin's being a cultural desert when its production of himself (to say nothing of his contemporaries Shaw, Wilde, Yeats, Synge, O'Casey, Connolly) offers its natural rebuttal. Nor is the important point really whether Mr Nairn at that point was right or wrong. One suspects that many of his opponents would secretly have believed that he was right, but he shouldn't have said it. Reading it nine years later, the most notable point is that it is written from such extraordinary pain.

And this, it seems to me, is one of the most important points on the interaction of socialism and nationalism. It is a cruel business for a reflective person. It means an identification with two great causes whose practice so often reduces the great theory to dreadful mockery. Socialism responds by taking refuge in the clouds, a temptation to which some essays in the Red Paper succumb, but not Mr Nairn's contribution. And the most genuine nationalists often suffer from a love for their country so deep that it expresses itself in a bitter scorn for the sanctimonious drivel uttered by more shallow minds in pursuit of easy hosannas.

Much of the formal noises about Scotland must seem to those whose love-for it is deepest as comparable to watching a drunken parent being cheered along the rake's progress by an audience of malicious enemies, shallow friends and, above all, parasites. I can understand how the alien intonations of myself in particular, and Mr Maxwell to a lesser degree, must have seemed like supporting noises from that entourage.

Mr Nairn's Red Paper piece has very wise words about internationalism; yet I am arguing that part of his mind is less internationalist than the minds of the more confident S.N.P. propagandists. Even in the Red Paper essay it is evident that the wound still exists. Mr Nairn mutters darkly about the "tartan monster" and his own previous effort to "wrestle" with it. What lies behind all of this is a very sensitive question. MacDiarmid, in fact, summarises it perfectly. We are fond of quoting his lines that the rose of all the world is not for him, only the little rose of Scotland that breaks the heart. It would be ludicrous to charge MacDiarmid, or Nairn for that matter, with any pervasive emnity to internationalism. These men have achieved nationalism in the truest sense, by taking a world perspective, by making the wrongs of so much of the suffering in the world their own, above all by writing with a universal relevance. But in both of them there is a capacity for heartbreak, and it is only Scotland which can deal that wound.

Ireland's Lessons and Example

The problem, in a sense, is unanswerable. The S.N.P. has the duty to arouse the Scottish people to a pride and a participation in Scotland. It was the task which Daniel O'Connell had to accomplish for the poverty-stricken masses of Ireland. In the process O'Connell did many great things — notably by nailing the colours of Irish nationalism to the international antislavery mast from which John Mitchel, Arthur Griffith and others later tried to tear them down — but he also enlisted the aid of Irish versions of the tartan monster.

It was not a green monster; he realised the need to cater to feelings of Irish respect for the royal connection, and Protestant worship of the Orange tradition. But it was monstrous and vulgar all the same; and it was not only an elitist dislike of popular tribunes which led Yeats to revile him. The coarseness and seeming buffoonery of O'Connell symbolised a degradation of the aesthetic ideal to Yeats.

Nairn and MacDiarmid are Marxists, and such elitism as they have is purely that from which no intellectual or artist can escape — it is what makes him what he is, and hence above the rest of us. Their ideals are great ones, as opposed to those of Yeats, whose politics were, in many respects, appalling. But one still has to remember that testimony of Auden that "mad Ireland hurt" Yeats "into poetry". And similarly the real Scottish artist or intellectual will have to express his very deep patriotism in terms which seem hurtful to people many of whom are doing the best they can, with far less linguistic facility.

I am a Johnny-come-lately, and it is, in a famous Irish phrase, easy to lie on another man's wound. In one sense I have yet to become a Scottish nationalist. I don't share Mr Nairn's pain — though I do share his disgust — at the prostitution of Scotland. In the case of Ireland, I do find I have parallel reactions. Indeed, on rereading his Red Paper piece I find I have angrily marked the errors on Ireland which it contains with a comparable annoyance to that which elicits his own anger at my nonsense, as he sees it, about Scotland.

On one level I am being pedantic and nationalistically sensitive; Mr Nairn had simply forgotten Ireland. But on another I can see my awareness that here is yet more nonsense added to the roaring cataract of bilge which the subject of Ireland seems to induce.

To indulge myself further, I can tell Mr Nairn that my wound is a much nastier one than his. Bilge about Ireland is destroying lives at this moment; bilge about Scotland has largely contented itself with whitewashing the hideous working and living conditions to which its people have been subjected. Bilge about Ireland actually resulted in the banning of innumerable books by Irish writers; bilge about Scotland simply ensured that many of its best books would be reviled and not read.

Tartan Rhetoric

In the earlier part of this essay I have made the obvious and accurate point that socialism and nationalism can cover a multitude of sins. The case of Mr Nairn reminds us that a great deal of nationalist rhetoric has already been employed to cover such sins; it has, indeed, been the alibi which robbed Scotland in the past of true socialism as well as true nationalism. Mr Nairn's essay has much of wisdom to say on this; Mr Nairn's wound is even more instructive.

It is obvious that the false nationalism which repels Mr Nairn is not, for the most part, the nationalism of the S.N.P. Being wounded, he will never quite be able to endure the S.N.P.'s more exotic rhetoric with the same fortitude which others can. I can make speeches about Scottish nationalism which would embarrass me horribly if I heard them being delivered about Irish nationalism.

It is one of the cruellest things for the most sensitive nationalists that the prostitution of their cause has been carried on so long as to debase the whole linguistic currency of nationalism. In saying this, the sufferer is quite capable of having his own moments of chauvinism; Mr Nairn's wrestling matches with the tartan monster occasionally show a sign of lack of total immunity to the monster's more subtle contagious germs. I may dislike listening to Irish chauvinistic speeches, but I can lapse into making one or two chauvinistic noises myself.

The real lesson of all of this is Mr Nairn's own. "To this day," he wrote in 1967, "a profoundly false, wish-fulfilling nostalgia remains the characteristic Scottish emotion." Well, to *this* day, it certainly doesn't. As he himself has shown elsewhere, Scottish nationalism has mercifully arisen on a mass level with very little obsessive domination by the past. It is not particularly Anglophobe. It is cheerful rather than resentful. It is confident rather than morose.

But he is right to stress that Scotland was led to acquiesce in cultural impoverishment, economic clientship, social class-polarisation and national obliteration by the serving of tartan pottage in horse-doctor's doses. I would say that, in fact, for all the tartan rhetoric that may creep into our election speeches in the S.N.P., there is a good deal of awareness that the tartan monster was our enemy.

105

In the most obvious reading of the matter, Mr Nairn will agree that the S.N.P. will certainly not settle for a "Prince of ₊Scotland" or some corresponding constitutional flummery in place of its demands. Nor will it assume that a free issue of tartans to the inhabitants of the Gorbals will solve their problems.

But the tartan monster could re-emerge for us in more subtle forms. After all, what the mass of Scotland once knew of nationalism was tartanry; we will have to be alert against its survival.

The Politics of Patriotism

I wrote the first section of this essay in Scotland; I wrote the middle in the U.S.A.; I am finishing it in Ireland. Conversations and observations in all three countries induce some feelings of optimism, and some of anxiety. In Ireland and in the U.S.A. formal expressions of patriotism now almost automatically induce a mixture of scepticism and nausea in their hearers. Look at a man displaying an American flag on his lapel and, you will be told, you are looking at a bigot or a crook. Mr Nixon's notorious team of public servants were great men for their mini-stars-and-stripes; so too are the most atrocious reactionaries devoted to the cult of St John Birch and comparable icons. As a result, innumerable Americans whom one knows to be dedicated to the deepest and noblest forms of patriotism automatically turn with disgust from any public expression of love of country. On any fair analysis their readiness to eradicate injustice in their society and make America a fair name once more is a far more praiseworthy outlook than that of those who would deny or defend what is wrong. But the reactionaries have usurped the ground of patriotism so thoroughly that debate simply cannot take place on that ground. However good the American Left's proof of its own patriotism are, the hypocricy of their enemies acts as a permanent injunction against their use of patriotic terms of reference.

In Ireland the situation is, if anything, worse. The Union Jack has for years been employed in Northern Ireland as a means for the humiliation of Roman Catholics and as a practical reminder to them that further humiliation is desirable. The tricolour, in the six counties, is a symbol of defiance of Unionism, and a comparable reminder that its votaries hope for the subordination of Unionists in a state which commands neither their affection nor their allegiance. By now, the extreme wings on both sides see the flags of the other as a promise of ultimate genocide. (It is worth stressing, for a world which gibbers about extremists, that the most dangerous extremists are those with extreme *fears*, not extreme ambitions: apart from anything else, they are much more numerous.)

In the Republic, the problem is not one of flag-waving. Patriotism has become a dirty word in another way. It has led directly, in its ultimate form not to an end to the Border but to the horror in the north. More visibly and more immediately it has accounted for a continuous process of cultural impoverishment and social retrogression — relatively speaking — in which tribal ideals have always been the great justification for obscurantism and annihilation of criticism. The Abbey riots against the plays of Synge and O'Casey, the opposition to radical social legislation, the justification of privilege for ecclesiastical and other special interests are all facets of this diamond.

Once again, the critic who questions the fraudulent patriotic impulses simply loses friends: embarrassed eyebrows are raised at his choice of a rhetoric soiled by chauvinism, and, even worse, he finds the ominous prospect of attracting "Left-wing" allies on the more intellectual fringes of the I.R.A. If patriotism has become an unspeakable virtue for the American Left, it is one whose utterance is really perilous for the Irish Left.

In the case of England, the situation is different. English nationalism, significantly enough, is common to all elements on the political spectrum; except that it is not called that. An English Socialist can permit himself to be quite noisily patriotic to an extent which would make his Irish or American counterpart cringe.

English Socialists who opposed entry into E.E.C. had no awkwardness at all about appealing to English sacred cornerstones (the colour of the cornerstones varied from those stressed by the Right, but it was not a drastic variance). Neither had their opponents. The Irish referendum on entry is not comparable to the British. But there is a comparison in the debates. Conor Cruise O'Brien could write that the Irish vote recorded the views of "quite a few people who, in their hearts, were frightened at the idea of being locked up alone in the cold, clammy dark, with Cathleen ni Houlihan and her memories of the dead".

The British verdict was no more a vote against nationalism in England than it was in Scotland and Wales. Indeed many of the most vociferous advocates of entry into E.E.C. have shown in their opposition to Scottish nationalism and in the style thereof, how fundamentally rooted in the ideology and rhetoric of English nationalism they remain. The problem about English nationalism is that the very factors which repel conscientious Irish and American Socialists from asserting their excellent nationalist credentials — self-righteousness, stress on moral superiority, insistence on national destiny, flirtation with imperial justifications for dominating persons of hostile views — are those to which English Socialists should give much more attention. To love England should not be to assume English answers the only answers.

As Professor V. G. Kiernan has shown,[10] it took English (and Scottish) Socialists a very long time to reach that conclusion on imperial questions. In some ways acceptance of the conclusion was more expressed than felt. In dealing with Scottish nationalism English Socialists still seem motivated by a gut-reaction that Big Brother knows best. In a sense I am making a bad case for the S.N.P. here in that I am arguing for a real inability on the part of English Socialists, in general, to come to terms as yet with their own nationalism. They show a common celebration of the doctrines, but not in a healthy form. Why should Scotland, a country strongly dominated by English influence, prove itself immune to comparable diseases?

Scottish Nationalism

Scottish nationalism did at one time find some expression in the distortion of British imperialism. John Buchan and innumerable less articulate Scottish military and political counterparts found in the empire a Greater Scotland where Scots could show the stuff they were made of by knocking the wogs on the head. Well, that joke is over. Scottish nationalism, now divested of its British imperial clothing, is learning the language of privation in place of that of luxuriant exploitation.

It is true that an independent Scotland offers the opportunity for Scots to exploit other Scots. And the only answer to this is not to concede a vital

H

battleground to our enemies by denying Scotland's right to independence, but rather to ensure that the independence is true, radical and real. It will have to be a Scotland in which those who claim to free their people must be personally responsible for guarding the vital freedoms of everyone in the new state. Otherwise, our independence is worthless. But we have a much better chance of guarding against injustice in a small territory where less can be hidden.

In an independent Scotland the diversity of the country acts as an insurance against the oppression of any one region over another. It is not an insurance that we can treat as a recipe for inaction. Still less can we permit the perpetuation of urban squalor, class exploitation, brutalising poverty and the innumerable sins which are now so comfortably placed at the door of the hapless incompetents who rule us at present.

The need for nationalists to make good on our claim that Scotland will solve her own problems is a political necessity as well as, more importantly, a moral one. And only with a sense of community needs and socialist equality can we carry such real nationalism into effect. Scotland without freedom for each individual from want, and fear, and degradation, and cultural stultification, is no freedom at all.

The S.N.P. must respond to Mr Nairn's challenge by giving a high place to culture in its agenda. And it cannot be an artificial place. Nor can it be one which involves a cultural dictatorship, with whatever high ideals. Culture thrives in dissent: we have much to learn from it, we have everything to lose by ignoring it or fearing it. Scotland gave the world a great generation in its enlightenment, none of whose leaders could be cited as advocates of Scottish independence. If unionism can produce another enlightenment, good luck to it.

7:84 will doubtless continue to lampoon us, as they have in the past, and we shall, I trust, continue to applaud and cheer it, as we have in the past.[11] The best of examples spur us on. Any S.N.P. person not inspired by Hugh MacDiarmid is in want of a vital nationalist component; yet Hugh MacDiarmid was expelled from our party before it was founded. It is irritating, certainly, to see bastions of opposition such as those of the university establishments: but the S.N.P. must not throw out the babies, however necessary it may be to change the bathwater, improve the soap and pension off Nannie.

The Radical Alternative

In all of this, my confidence may seem a little naïve. And I lack demonstrable proof. All I can say is that I know my party, and I believe its impulses are radical. I dislike and disapprove of certain views of certain members on certain issues; and *vice versa*. But the character of the party is radical. It is a party of the present, as no other party in Scotland is. It has a capacity to learn from the past; its urgent need of cultural revitalisation is partly caused by a duty to deepen and enlarge that process; but it is not an involvement with the past to provide ammunition for whining.

The roots of many of its members lie in socialist ideals, notably the C.N.D. movement, and its implacable opposition to murderous nuclear arsenals gives it a better title to be socialist in the truest sense than may be said for many so-called socialist parties. Its response to the economic and environmental questions dominating Scotland at present has to be radical. There simply is no alternative.

The demand for our own oil means an end of oil in pawn to multi-national corporations, whether or not one of the three balls on the pawnbroker's sign is British-made, or the pawnbroker's boy gets drunk once a week and sings "The Red Flag".

We have to create a situation where our remarkable asset — patriotism which still remains open to the vocabulary of a Scottish socialist without loss of his socialism — can be employed to show that the language of patriotism means the language of socialism. And in addition to showing that the truest independence will be a socialist independence, we will also prove that a socialism based on Scotland is one of the fullest international consciousness, in place of the pathetic internationalism of our opponents whose horizons are limited to London (a trading outpost of Wall Street and Texas).

1 Gordon Brown, editor, *The Red Paper on Scotland*, Edinburgh 1975.
2 Bob Tait, "The Left, the S.N.P. and the Oil", *The Red Paper*, ibid, pp 125-133.
3 Jim Sillars, "Land Ownership and Land Nationalisation", *The Red Paper*, ibid, pp 254-261.
4 James Young, "The Rise of Scottish Socialism", *The Red Paper*, ibid, pp 282-288.
5 Henry George, *Progress and Poverty: An Inquiry into the Cause of Industrial Depressions, and of an Increase in Want with Increase in Wealth: the Remedy*, London, 1883.
6 John McEwen, "Highland Landlordism", *The Red Paper*, ibid, pp 262-269.
7 Ray Burnett, "Socialists and the S.N.P.", *The Red Paper*, ibid, pp 108-124.
8 Tom Nairn, "Old Nationalism and New Nationalism", *The Red Paper*, ibid, pp 22-57.
9 Tom Nairn, "Festival of the Dead", *New Statesman*, 1st September 1967.
10 V. G. Kiernan, *The Lords of Human Kind*, London, 1966.
11 See John McGrath (The 7:84 Theatre Company): "The Cheviot, the Stag and the Black, Black Oil".

Question:

The independent monthly political review for Scotland.

Lively and controversial, *Q* is essential reading for intelligent discussion on the fast-changing political scene in Scotland.

Available at all good newsagents in Scotland. Subscription rates for a year, including postage: U.K. and Eire £3.30; Europe £6.60 air mail, £5.00 surface; rest of the world £8.40 air mail, £5.00 surface.

30p monthly

Palingenesis Press Ltd.
56 Dean Street, Edinburgh, EH4 1LQ